A Very Private Practice

An investigation into private fostering

Terry Philpot

BAAF
ADOPTION
& FOSTERING

Published by
**British Agencies for Adoption & Fostering
(BAAF)**
Skyline House
200 Union Street
London SE1 0LX
www.baaf.org.uk

Charity registration 275689

© Terry Philpot and BAAF, 2001

British Library Cataloguing in Publication Data
A catalogue record for this book is available
from the British Library

ISBN 1 903699 05 3

Editorial and project management by
Shaila Shah, BAAF
Cover photograph by John Birdsall Photography,
posed by models
Designed by Andrew Haig & Associates
Typeset and printed by Aldgate Press, London

BAAF is an independent organisation promoting
the highest standards of child-centred policies
and services for children separated from their
family of origin.

This report is dedicated to the memory of Victoria Climbié, a privately fostered child, whose tragic death may yet provoke a change in the law to offer greater protection to all those children who find themselves similarly cared for.

Author's acknowledgements

It is impossible for me to thank all those who assisted in the research carried out for this report. I spoke to more than 30 people and visited different parts of the country to follow up some of those conversations. Those to whom I spoke were mainly working in local authorities but also in the voluntary sector and elsewhere. Many are named here, although some people are, of necessity, anonymously quoted.

I would especially like to acknowledge the assistance I received from Brendan McGrath, Private Fostering Co-ordinator, Gloucestershire, who has an infectious enthusiasm for his subject, and from whom I suffered an *embarrassement de richesse* in the amount of information which he offered. He also drew my attention to historical references to private fostering much earlier than the case of the notorious Mrs Walters in 1870. I also wish to acknowledge the indispensable help of Beverley Clarke, health visitor and team adviser, Lambeth, Southwark and Lewisham Health Authority, who has done so much to promote the needs of black children who are privately fostered. She gave me many ideas and much information, written and verbal. Joy Okoye, a leading barrister on these issues, opened my eyes to the tragedy of parents who, unwittingly, find that in asking only that someone else cares for their child, too often lose those children through adoption proceedings. Three others who deserve special mention are Heather Reid, Joint Director of the N'Deagainsia Project, Angus Geddes, Fostering Development Officer, Swindon Social Services Department, and Cherie Talbot, Training Manager, Fostering Network, and a former registered local authority foster carer. Beverley Clarke, Angus Geddes, Brendan McGrath and Cherie Talbot are members of BAAF's Private Fostering Special Interest Group, as are some others to whom I have spoken. The PFSIG has succeeded over the years in continuing to exert pressure for change and to keep the issue of private fostering alive.

I would also like to thank "Adenike" who kindly allowed me to retell her painful experiences.

Acknowledgement must also be made of "Patricia", "Adjua" and "Robert", who told me their story.

Sir William Utting, whose 1997 report, *People Like Us*, has helped to keep this issue on the boil when it might easily have disappeared, kindly agreed to write the Foreword. Everyone in child care owes Sir William an enormous debt which goes far beyond the issues which affect private fostering.

At BAAF, I have relied on the ever cheerful support, advice and help of its Chief Executive, Felicity Collier, who commissioned the report, and also that of Pete Wrighton, BAAF's consultant on private fostering. They and Deborah Cullen, BAAF's legal adviser, helpfully read the manuscript. Shaila Shah, BAAF's Head of Communications, is responsible for the excellent design and editing of this report which I know makes it all the more readable.

Last but not least, thanks are due to the Stanley Smith Charitable Trust who funded this work.

The opinions and ultimate responsibility for this report (and any errors contained therein!) are mine but I am sure that all those to whom I spoke will recognise their collective and beneficial influence on the final report. The recommendations have been developed by BAAF.

The author

Terry Philpot is a writer on social policy and was formerly Editor and Editor in Chief of *Community Care*. He has written and edited several books, including *Action for Children*; *Values and Visions: Changing ideas in services for people with learning difficulties* (with Linda Ward); *Sweet Charity: The work and role of voluntary organisations* (with Chris Hanvey); *Caring and Coping: A guide to social services* (with Anthony Douglas); and *Political Correctness and Social Work*. His latest book, *Adoption: Changing lives, changing times* (with Anthony Douglaš) will be published next year by Routledge. He is a trustee of the Centre for Policy on Ageing and RPS-Rainer and a member of the advisory committee for the Economic and Social Research Council's Growing Older Programme. He has won several awards for journalism.

Contents

PRIVATE FOSTERING SPECIAL INTEREST GROUP

The Private Fostering Special Interest Group facilitated by Pete Wrighton (Consultant, BAAF) and Marcia Spencer (ex-Black Issues Project Manager, BAAF) has over the years, continued to exert pressure for change and to keep the issues surrounding private fostering in the public eye. Below is a list of core members. For more information, contact Pete Wrighton, PO Box 129, Bristol B59 3AB. Tel: 0117 962 6567.

Iris Amoah, Social Worker
   London Borough of Newham
Amma Anane-Agyei
   Specialist Social Worker/Trainer/Consultant
   London
Beverley Clarke, Health Visitor, London
Heather Clacy, Social Worker
   Kent Social Services
Angus Geddes, Fostering Development Officer
   Swindon Social Services
Bob Holman, Writer, Glasgow
Hale Longpet, Strategic Development worker
   Bread Youth Project, Bristol
Sue Lynch, Social Worker, Essex Social Services
Yvonne Martins, Social Worker
   London Borough of Newham
Brendan McGrath, Private Fostering Co-ordinator
   Gloucestershire Social Services
Desma Melbourne, Social Worker
   North Warwickshire Children & Families Service
Theresa Shiyanbola, Director
   African Women's Welfare Association
   Ayoka Project
Cherie Talbot, Training Manager
   Fostering Network
Representatives from:
   Department of Health; Nigerian High
   Commission; Thomas Coram Research Unit

NOTE

This report is concerned mainly with private fostering in England and the legislation which affects it, although there is no reason to think that what is described here is any different from elsewhere in the UK. However, there are some references to Scotland because of the reports of the amount of private fostering among its Chinese population. The responsibilities of Scottish and English local authorities with regard to private fostering are very similar. But, with the passing of the Regulation of Care (Scotland) Act 2001, Scottish authorities, unlike their English and Welsh counterparts, will have to register as providers of services. However, also, unlike in England and Wales, in Scotland, the service which Scottish authorities offer in respect of private fostering will be subject to inspection by the Scottish Commission for the Regulation of Care. In England the Social Services Inspectorate can inspect such services – and has twice done so – but it is not required to.

All the stories related here, whether in the main text or as case studies, have been anonymised by changing both names and areas of the country mentioned. The exception are those related in a programme on private fostering in the television series, *Black Bag*, where the interviewees chose to be identified. The stories are used mainly to show the situations in which children can be placed. Some, however, illustrate the attitudes of local authorities.

Foreword
Sir William Utting

The report of the review of safeguards for children living away from home (*People Like Us*, 1997) devoted a substantial chapter to foster care that included only three pages on private fostering. This was largely because facts and knowledge about the subject were alarmingly scarce. The lack of reliable information was itself a serious criticism of the existing system of regulation. Indeed, regulation appeared to work so haphazardly that it could not in any meaningful sense be characterised as a system.

One of the review's general conclusions was that there should be a consistent, minimum level of safeguards for children across all the settings in which they might live away from home. Determined abusers seek out any sector in which controls and external scrutiny are weak, and incompetent carers are naturally drawn to areas in which staff selection and supervision are unknown. It was plain to the review that private fostering was among the least controlled and most open to abuse of all the environments in which children lived away from home.

The review was by no means alone in this judgement. Interested and knowledgeable organisations thrust this opinion upon us in evidence. Recent reports (the latest in a worrying sequence over the years) by the Race Equality Unit and the Social Services Inspectorate had emphasised the vulnerability of those children who were both cut off from their parents and placed

It was plain to the review that private fostering was among the least controlled and most open to abuse of all the environments in which children lived away from home.

with strangers whose antecedents were unknown.

Another perplexing inconsistency was the contrast in regulation between day care and private fostering. Childminders and other providers of day care operate within a system of registration based on their fitness for the task, which is reinforced by inspection and supported by training and other practical help. Yet the safety of privately fostered children depends upon the exercise of local authority discretion triggered by a declaration by the carers themselves. It is perverse for children who live with strangers to receive a lower level of protection than those who live in their own homes and go out to care on a daily basis.

The review concluded that the current situation should no longer be tolerated. It consequently recommended that private foster carers should be required to seek approval and registration from their local authority, and that non-compliance should become a criminal offence.

There are two major difficulties in putting this into practice. Private foster care covers a wide variety of social situations; a system of supervision to protect the most vulnerable – which is in my view both necessary and unavoidable – might be unduly onerous if applied rigidly to all.

The second difficulty is in motivating and resourcing local authorities to take seriously a responsibility to which most have, for perhaps understandable reasons, afforded low priority in the past. Both can be resolved: the former by central guidance that differentiates between the contexts in which private fostering takes place, and the latter by ensuring the supply of adequately trained and experienced personnel.

Terry Philpot's report provides a timely and comprehensive account of the history and current state of private fostering. His recommendations chart a clear course for the future. Surely – at last – now is the time to bring private fostering into the ring of acknowledged, regulated, and supported services for children, and to provide a group of largely forgotten children with the protection given to all the others who live away from home.

October 2001

Surely – at last – now is the time to bring private fostering into the ring of acknowledged, regulated, and supported services for children, and to provide a group of largely forgotten children with the protection given to all the others who live away from home.

1 **Private lives**

In 1997, in the wake of the publication of a report by the African Family Advisory Service on private fostering, BAAF Adoption and Fostering issued a press release calling for the registration of private foster carers. Felicity Collier, Chief Executive, said: 'We cannot wait for a tragedy to happen.' But we did. Three years and one month later, eight-year-old Victoria Climbié, in the "care" of her great-aunt Marie Thérèse Kouao, and Karl Manning, her great-aunt's partner, a stranger to the child, and 3,000 miles from her parents in the Ivory Coast, was systematically beaten and tortured and left to die of hypothermia and starvation.

Some parents will always need to make use of private foster care. But the needs of their children for support, protection and a healthy physical and emotional development are no different from those of any other child.

That was not the only example of the fearful symmetry which afflicts private fostering. More than 25 years ago, Bob Holman in *Trading in Children* (Holman, 1973), which remains the classic, major and most thorough study of the subject, concluded that registration had to be introduced into a market in children even less regulated then than it is now. And yet, days after life sentences were pronounced on Victoria Climbié's murderers, Holman found himself writing again – this time in a national newspaper – to make the same plea (Holman, 2001).

The inquiry into the circumstances leading to the death of Victoria, now being conducted by Lord Laming, may recommend that the law be strengthened to make unregistered private fostering illegal. Certainly, everyone in childcare sees the child's death as the tragic justification for such a change. That is, everyone except the Department of Health which has continued to cling to the arguments which it has propounded for more than the last dozen years. These are that the law is sufficient as it stands and it is up to local authorities to enforce it; and that private fostering is essentially an arrangement between the parents and the carers, and, as such, the prime responsibility for the welfare of those children rests with the parents. These arguments are dealt with at length later in this report.

However, should the death of Victoria Climbié, coming as it does after several years of agitation for changes – most recently *People Like Us*, the report of the Utting inquiry (Utting, 1997) – prove to be a Damascene experience for the Government, then the wheel will truly have turned full circle. For it was the case of Mrs Walters, in 1870, who was tried and executed for the murder of several children, which led the Select Committee on the Protection of Infant Life to produce a report in 1871 detailing the uncovering of a widespread system of "baby farming", as private fostering was then known. The report led to the passing of the Infant Life Protection Act 1872, the first recognition of a public duty in this area.

Set apart by law
In *Trading in Children*, Holman sums up succinctly the essential transaction which private fostering involves: 'Parents require a service, foster carers offer a service – the two sides contact each other, negotiate the terms and the goods (the children) change hands.'

For various reasons, which are explained in this report, some parents will always need to make use of private foster care. But the needs of their children for support, protection and a healthy physical and emotional development are no different from those of any other child. And yet these children are set apart by the law and dealt with separately from almost all other children who are either in the care of a local authority or who are in the care of people other than their parents – children at school, nursery school or playgroup, or children in the care of childminders. While nannies are not registered or approved, parents can, at least, ascertain an idea of their competence by ensuring that those whom they employ hold the National Nursery Examination Board Qualification; also, children looked after by nannies remain at home.

All children looked after by a local authority are, by definition, vulnerable; this is not so for all children looked after by other kinds of carers and nor is it automatically the case for privately fostered children, though very large numbers of them are vulnerable and are potentially subject to harm.

People Like Us was explicitly concerned with 'the safeguards for children living away from home'. The government response was, on the whole, massively encouraging – it pledged itself to the Quality Protects initiative; it pumped £380 million over three-and-a-half years into a new Children's Services Special Grant; it sought to promote the child's voice with another three-year grant of £450,000. It made practical commitments to staff training, care leavers, and in health,

education and boarding schools, the penal system and criminal justice. It was concerned with inter-agency working and stopping dangerous people from working with children. Few, if any, government responses to an inquiry report on a single, albeit large and important policy issue, have been so wide-ranging and met with such open-hearted support from those who will be responsible for the transformation of that service – those who daily work in it and manage it. And yet the one major recommendation which the Government refused to accept was that for registration of those caring for children who are privately fostered. It did so on the well-worn grounds that:

It does not consider that a new system of regulation is necessary as there is already a wide range of offences associated with private fostering and the Government does not believe that it would be right to extend them further.
(Department of Health, 1998)

Its concession to what it had been told about private fostering, and the claim of the Utting inquiry that those children were particularly vulnerable to abuse, was to add:

However, it [the Government] will take steps in 1999 to enforce the current regulations for private fostering more effectively. This action will include an awareness campaign and will be targeted at the most vulnerable groups of children. When parliamentary time allows, legislation will be introduced to target private fostering regulations at placements (whether singular or consecutive) lasting more than 42 days. The Government will also work with a range of agencies to draw up a code of practice for language schools bringing children from overseas.
(Department of Health, 1998)

Yet even these commitments, inadequate though they were, were not to be realised.

First, the "awareness campaign" arrived this year, two years later than was promised, in the shape of a leaflet aimed at professional staff. The Social Services Inspectorate's inspections of private fostering in 1993 (Department of Health, 1994) came to the conclusion that 'information about private fostering, and the requirement to notify local authorities of placements was virtually unknown to the general public'. It is, thus, safe to say that the Government's latest effort will leave the public's ignorance intact. Second, whatever might have been the effect of the 42-day legislation will never be known. Parliamentary time did not, in the event, apparently allow. Third, the code of practice for language schools was never published.

Such a response (or the lack of it) proved to be a sorry addendum to the positive, otherwise comprehensive and enormously influential response of the Government to almost every other aspect of the Utting report.

Looking at parallels

When considering the legal position of those who privately foster and what should be the responsibilities of local authorities with regard to the care of the children, realistically, the parallel is with those children who are looked after by others by the wish of their parents. All children looked after by a local authority are, by definition, vulnerable; this is not so for all children looked after by other kinds of carers and nor is it automatically the case for privately fostered children, though very large numbers of them are vulnerable and are potentially subject to harm. But given the resources available to local authorities, a degree of discretion on the part of social workers would be necessary were notifications to rise dramatically with the advent of registration, as they most certainly would. For example, for social workers to assess thoroughly all the homes to which every language student is assigned, or where every teenager in conflict with their parents goes, would make the whole system unworkable and

The numbers of children privately fostered are much greater than is currently recorded and there are resource implications.

would hinder the much more stringent work needed to be carried out for the large numbers of other privately fostered children who are vulnerable. Perhaps other agencies could lessen the burden on local authorities. Boarding schools are now registered and inspected. Some of them offer, as part of their service, an assurance to parents of the quality of the homes in which their pupils will be placed during holidays if it is not possible for them to spend that time with their parents. Likewise, in Oxfordshire, language schools, in co-operation with the Social Services Department, have taken on this responsibility, although language schools themselves are not subject to inspection.

It is not unnatural – indeed, it is inevitable – for local authorities to make priorities, to tackle those circumstances in their areas which they find most acute, and to attempt to meet the needs of those groups in their population whom they believe to be most at risk. For example, Hampshire has done hardly any work with language schools, a number of which it has within its borders, because it has given priority to the very large numbers of West African children who have come to live as privately fostered children in the county.

However, as this report will show, even though there is irrefutable evidence that privately fostered children are, mostly, a group at risk, they are also a group who lack protection through a combination of inaction by both central and local government.

As the Utting report (1997) pointed out, there is also a world of difference between parents

We know very little about privately fostered children or the care they receive or the people who care for them. They are hidden just as Victoria Climbié was hidden.

who make arrangements with friends and neighbours to look after their children for a period while, for example, they move house, and parents who give their children into the care of strangers, with only the most cursory of investigations. Utting sees vast risks in these latter situations – but in any private fostering arrangement there are, at least, minimum risks.

The numbers of children privately fostered are much greater than is currently recorded and there are resource implications. Local authorities are beset by many urgencies but that is no reason to pretend, as many social services departments do, that vast under-reporting of private foster placements means that there is little or nothing to do.

In 1991, Carol Woollard (1991) remarked that the numerous structural changes in the NHS – she was writing with health service staff in mind – meant that that 'might mean that there is little time or energy left for attention to be paid to this comparatively neglected group of children'. Here, again, nothing changes. Reorganisations in both health and social services have continued apace since Woollard made her prediction and now, in the cause of

the Labour Government's modernisation programme for health and social services, even more radical changes are afoot. Primary care trusts are to be created, care trusts will come into being, and social services departments may well disappear eventually. Those, like children in private foster care, who are already way at the back of the queue at the moment, are even less likely to be noticed in the flurry of reorganisation that comes with restructuring. But Whitehall-induced restructuring aside, too often local authorities appear to be in the grip of perpetual internal reorganisations. Indeed, one senior manager in London, with responsibility for private fostering, excused his authority's lack of action by telling me: 'We have been preoccupied with the [internal] reorganisation.'

While registration would undoubtedly increase the numbers known to local authorities, other local authority policies could have unforeseen consequences. For example, if a local authority were to introduce charges for children voluntarily in its care, as some already have and others plan to do, this might cause a parent to see private foster care as a better option financially.

We know very little about privately fostered children or the care they receive or the people who care for them. They are hidden just as Victoria Climbié was hidden. But the trail that leads from Mrs Walters' pathetic little victims to Victoria Climbié's horrific death in London 130 years later confirms, yet again, the truth of Heinrich Heine's dictum that what we learn from history is that we do not learn from history.

2 Points of law

The Children Act 1989 largely took over from the Foster Children Act 1980, which was a consolidating Act, the definition of private fostering – the care of a child up to the age of 16 (18 if disabled or who has special needs) by a person for 28 days or more who is not the child's parent or relative. The Act defined who are relatives for these purposes: grandparents, siblings, step-parents, aunts and uncles or other persons having parental responsibility.

The two major changes ushered in by the Children Act 1989 were the duty placed on both carer and parent to notify an intention to place a child in private foster care, and limiting the numbers of children whom a carer could foster to three.

The two major changes ushered in by the Children Act 1989 were the duty placed on both carer and parent to notify an intention to place a child in private foster care, and limiting the numbers of children whom a carer could foster to three.

During the passage of the then Children Bill, amendments to include pre-placement inquiries and the imposition of a duty on local authorities to consider the privately fostered child's religion, race and cultural background were lost (Atkinson and Horner, 1990). However, in a statement to the Commons on 23 October 1989, David Mellor, Minister of State, Department of Health, said that the regulations would address these issues and went on:

We expect authorities as part of their pre-placement inquiries and duty to give advice to foster carers on the children's needs arising from their racial origin and cultural background.

He also stated:

I am glad to make clear that local authorities' powers are to be extended to give them the power to prohibit any private fostering placement where the foster carer or the accommodation is unsuitable or the placement is prejudicial to the child's welfare.

The Bill as passed into law stated:

It shall be the duty of every local authority to satisfy themselves that the welfare of children who are privately fostered in their area is being satisfactorily safeguarded and promoted and to secure that such advice is given to them as appears necessary to the authority to be needed.

The regulations accompanying the Act imposed a duty on local authorities to visit at a minimum of specified intervals. This was formerly at the local authorities' discretion (Department of Health, 1991).

And yet the Children Act should be viewed and used in its entirety and applied to all children who come within its ambit. To take a very obvious example, transracial placements can have very damaging consequences for many privately fostered West African children (the largest group of children who are looked after in this way). But while the Act places a responsibility on local authorities to have regard for a child's racial, cultural and religious background when considering placements, this seems not to have much influence when it comes to privately fostered children.

For the most part, local authorities have done very little for children who are privately fostered, hampered, as they are, first, by the demands on them for caring for children who are looked after, and second, by their not knowing where most privately fostered children are cared for or by whom. Local authorities can take, what Atkinson and Horner (1990) call, a "proactive" or "reactive" approach – they can either actively seek to uncover private fostering arrangements; provide a service by offering adequate assessment; maintain an unofficial register in the absence of a statutorily required one; offer training to carers; and, generally draw those carers into a partnership. Or they can wait until notified of arrangements and offer the minimum possible. Those that do anything, tend to do the latter (ADSS, 2001).

LOCAL AUTHORITY DUTIES

Local authorities' duties are to

- receive notifications from parents, carers and third parties;

- assess the suitability of the placement;

- visit the child in line with statutory requirements;

- ensure that carers are aware of the child's racial, cultural, linguistic and religious needs and are helped to meet them;

- offer advice and support to parents, carers and the children included in private fostering arrangements;

- assess applications for exemptions from the limit of fostering three children; and

- consider the need for specific requirements and prohibitions.

3 Impressions and estimates

What we know about private fostering is how little we know. In 1991, the Department of Health ceased collecting statistics because of the inaccuracy caused by the low number of notifications.

In 1988, the then Department of Health and Social Security estimated that there were 2,127 children being privately fostered in England and Wales. This was 30 fewer than the previous year and 1,000 less than in 1984. Yet the now defunct African Family Advisory Service did not consider at that time that the figures were growing less; indeed, they said, the opposite was the case. They used the evidence of the number of advertisements appearing in *Nursery World* (then the main public recruitment base for private foster carers). In 1987/88, there were 819 advertisements, against 614 the year before and 469 in 1984/5 (Atkinson and Horner, 1990). AFAS even qualified their inferences by supporting a much earlier writer, Leisham (1980), who, writing about the Nigerian family in Britain, said that there was an informal network of communication between families and that the numbers of advertisements did not represent the total number of children available on the private fostering market.

What we know about private fostering is how little we know. In 1991, the Department of Health ceased collecting statistics because of the inaccuracy caused by the low number of notifications.

Calculating the numbers
In 1991, AFAS, using a survey of 12 local authorities, claimed that there were 6–9,000 children, mainly under the age of five, in private foster care (quoted, Woollard, 1991). How it came by this figure is interesting given the conjectural nature of many estimations and the vast under-reporting since then. AFAS identified the 12 local authorities reporting the highest number of notifications to the DoH. It then investigated the number of non-notifications in those areas by carrying out household visits and, on the basis of those findings, extrapolated nationally. This is as near as anyone has ever come to arriving at anything like a properly calculated figure on a sophisticated basis. However, given that at that time concern was most focused on West African children and there was concern about widening the net to include other groups of children, like those coming to language schools, this figure is really about West African children. Thus, that being so, the numbers of children privately fostered are considerably larger.

The Utting report (Utting, 1997) says that in Wales, in 1994, 29 children were recorded in 27 foster homes. The report's estimate of 11,000 children privately fostered (against 35,000 with local authority-approved foster carers) in 1997 is another which appears to hark back to the AFAS figures in the absence of any more recent and reliable data. Brendan McGrath, Private Fostering Co-ordinator, Gloucestershire County Council, has calculated a similar figure. His 11,000, to which he attaches a query as if to imply that there may be more, derives from a variety of published statistics and estimates (McGrath, 2001a).

While West African children are not the only group of children who are privately fostered, although they may be the largest, Carol Woollard (1991) quotes an unpublished MSc thesis (Nesbitt, 1990) which found that 40 per cent of West African children in the researcher's sample entering school at five had experienced "a fostering situation" at some time. Given the context in which this is reported, the clear implication is that all or at least a majority of these children had been privately fostered.

AFAS's 1997 study was a more localised analysis of figures. The organisation visited and studied three local authorities – Kent, Shropshire and Hampshire – having surveyed ten. Self-returns of a proforma sent by one area office in the study to *known* foster carers revealed that there were 42 children privately fostered in 27 homes. But even here, when AFAS spoke to health visitors, who are more likely to be able to identify private foster carers than social workers, it stated that the health visitors believed, through patients registered with GPs, that they were in contact with a larger number of privately fostered children who were often unknown to social services.

Insofar as figures in this area can be given any credibility at all, it is interesting to look at earlier official statistics. Holman (1973) quotes Home Office figures based on the returns from the then local authority children's departments (predecessors of social services departments). These show that notifications increased substantially over the decade 1961– 69: in 1961 there were 6,780 notifications, rising to 8,038 in 1963, 10,600 in 1966 and 10,907 in 1969. Interestingly, more than 30 years later, only now is the Department of Health starting to quote similar figures for private placements, notified or not.

Recent exercises

There have been two surveys carried out this year (2001). The first was by the Association of Directors of Social Services which contacted its 179 members in England and Wales (ADSS, 2001). There was a 41 per cent (71) response rate. Forty-eight of the respondents said that they recorded the number of private fostering arrangements in their authority's area. (This is less than a third of all English and Welsh social services departments.) The cases ranged from 0–50 with an average of seven recorded private

fostering arrangements across the 47 authorities which provided figures. The report comments: 'However, there was no time period specified so the figures could be inaccurate if they cover different time spans.' Eight of the authorities estimated the full extent of private fostering arrangements in their authority. The estimates were 50, 30–45, upto 30, 20–30, less than 20, 10, 10 and four cases. Several said that it would be very difficult to estimate figures and that these were very much based on guess work. The ADSS comments: 'These estimates are not very reliable, as there was little or no evidence to support them.' Unsurprisingly, the report concludes that 'the extent of private fostering is impossible to estimate from the results of this survey'.

'The extent of private fostering is impossible to estimate from the results of this survey.'

In parenthesis, it is worth noting that the ADSS came up against the same problems as the Department of Health inspection of 1993 (Department of Health, 1994). The DoH's attempt to inspect a sample of six cases in each of the three local authorities under its microscope – Dorset, Stockport and Enfield – illustrated graphically the problems involved in even finding enough cases for so modest an exercise. One authority had six cases. These were the only ones known to it. All the children were white and while that may have been typical of the private fostering in that area, it is, of course, not typical of private fostering nationally. Another authority could only provide two cases from a population of more than 270,000 people, of whom 17,000 were under five years of age, more than 57,000 were aged 0–18 and 14 per cent of the total (36,315) were from minority ethnic communities. The third authority had 46 children placed with 29 carers in a population of 645,000, of whom 126,315 were aged under 18.

'There is a big gap between what we know and the reality… There is a gross under-reporting of the figures.'

The other study this year is based on the inspection carried out between December 2000 and March 2001 by the Social Services Inspectorate. This involved an in-depth inspection of five local authorities' arrangements for dealing with private fostering and an inspection of eight more authorities' policies and practices of fostering generally, with reference to private fostering. The inspection report has yet to be published but it is believed that the information gathered will be again insufficient to offer anything like an accurate estimation of the extent of private fostering.

The Department of Heath's pamphlet for professionals, *Private Fostering: A cause for concern*, states: 'It is estimated that about 10,000 children in England and Wales are privately fostered' (Department of Health, 2001). This figure, which is unreferenced, can only be an extrapolation of the estimate by AFAS. More curiously, the accompanying letter from Denise Platt, the Chief Inspector of Social Services, refers to 'the estimated 8,000–10,000 children'. The DoH pamphlet also says that 'it is likely that more than 50 per cent of private foster placements are not notified'. It is difficult to see where this figure could come from given that, while local authorities do have numbers for notifications (inadequate though that information is), that would be no guide to knowing how many they do not know about. Indeed, were the 50 per cent of unnotified cases reliable, it might mean, on the basis of the figures we do have, that the numbers are much smaller than we think!

Seeking to estimate impressionistically also illustrates how unreliable information sources can be. I asked three people said to have a responsibility in their local authority for private fostering if they could tell me how many private foster placements there were in their areas. All said they could not. A fourth inquiry elicited that the person could but, of course, she was referring only to known cases. In a fifth authority, a London borough, the senior officer responsible said he 'thought' there were three or four

families but suspected, from knowledge of his own cultural background (he was African-Caribbean), that there were many more. On the south coast, one person told me she knew of two cases, one of which was long standing (the child was nine and came to the carer's home when he was a baby). But a colleague from a neighbouring authority said: 'We are not in a position where we confidently believe we know them all – that's why we have the need to keep professionals and public constantly informed about the issue.' (These two authorities, both relatively small and with main towns that share newspapers, are planning a joint advertising and awareness campaign.)

In a north-eastern authority, the manager of the children and families team contacted 100 social workers in May to ask if they knew of any private foster carers. She received no response. She told me that she thought that there might be six and suspected that when the children came to the authority's notice it was not through notification but under other guises.

Fourteen years ago, a shire county recorded 49 carers and 43 children, numbers that fell 11 years ago to 23 and 35, respectively. They were concentrated mainly in one town, which has since become a unitary authority. Now, one social worker, who has worked in the field of private fostering all that time, says he personally knows of six privately fostered black children as well as some white teenagers, although the authority has only two private foster placements on its books. These falls can be attributed to two things: first, the unitary council did not carry on the shire authority's proactive work, and there is also poor recording. The latter was because when a new IT system was installed, there was no code to record private foster care!

Lincolnshire had 11 notifications (September 2001) but, as Margaret Reid, Reviewing Manager, told me: 'There is a big gap between what we know and the reality... There is a gross under-reporting of the figures.' A year previously there had been 15 notifications and the fall was largely attributable to adolescents returning to their families after a domestic dispute caused them to live elsewhere. The majority of the existing 11 cases are black children of student parents living in London. Historically, these children have marked out Lincolnshire's private fostering and it is believed that there were at one time 40 to 50 private fostering cases. Why the numbers have fallen is not known, although better notification in the past might account for it. Most of the black children live in one part of the county where a man acts as a broker between parents and carers. He advises them to notify the council.

Hampshire presents an interesting example of the problems of dealing with figures. While it lost Portsmouth and Southampton as a result of local government reorganisation, the majority of the West African children privately fostered have always been at Leigh Park, a large overspill estate in Havant, which remains within Hampshire's boundaries. It was believed that at one time there were 500 privately fostered children living there. In 1990 the number was put at 200. Again, at one time, there were alleged to be 200 private carers, a number which dropped to 50 in the mid-90s. An internal report to the council in 1993 put the number at 114 children, 95 of whom were of West African origin, and more than half of whom were below school age (Hampshire County Council, 1993).

The authority appointed a specialist black social worker under the Foster Care Act 1980. It published publicity material, as it still does, and worked with the children to prepare them to rejoin their families. It also worked with the local authorities in London from where the children came to plan their entry or re-entry into local schools. When the social worker retired, another, who was white, was appointed to take her place.

But today, however, there are ten placements on the authority's books in Havant and half a dozen elsewhere in the county. No-one can explain the dramatic fall in the figures.

4 A parental responsibility

Not a great deal is known about the parents of many of the privately fostered children and no study has looked at their motives in any depth since Holman's *Trading in Children* appeared in 1973. The parents of overseas students at language schools very probably expect that the schools make satisfactory arrangements in this country and thus their responsibility is limited to allowing their children to take part in the course.

We do know, though, quite a lot about the situation in which West African parents find themselves and some of this may apply to other parents in the situation where work or study makes caring for one's child difficult. While Holman (1973) said that the majority of the West African parents he studied were mainly students, it is possible that there is a new generation of West Africans who have settled here, mainly now to work rather than study.

Not a great deal is known about the parents of many of the privately fostered children and no study has looked at their motives in any depth since Holman's *Trading in Children* appeared in 1973.

The AFAS study (1997) could reveal very little about the parents and said that the social workers to whom it spoke rarely met them and then, usually, only when care proceedings or wardships were planned or under way.

A little knowledge

Only slightly more is known about private foster carers – again, Holman's is the most thorough investigation. However, the African Family Advisory Service (1997) found two foster carers over the age of 70. The television programme, *Black Bag* (1997), interviewed 75-year-old-widower, Keith Francis, who was caring for two black boys, aged nine and ten, who came to him and his wife (who had died three years previously) when they were babies. I was also told of a foster father who was in his 60s and who had a heart condition. His wife was not appreciably younger. The earlier AFAS report (1991) had also found four private foster carers who had experienced significant difficulties in raising their own children; a foster father who had been convicted of indecent assault; another with a conviction for violence; two foster families who had had their application to be local authority foster carers rejected; and one foster family whose own child had been received into care. AFAS's evidence in its later report (1997) was that most carers were approaching middle age. In Kent it found that 42 foster carers had an average age of 51. The eight case studies which AFAS recorded showed that all carers but one had teenage or adult children of their own. All the carers lived in council housing, several had husbands who were unemployed and of the husbands who worked, all were in manual and semi-skilled occupations.

The payments private foster carers can receive may not seem much but can be significant in terms of family income. Certainly, the income is much lower than the allowances which local authorities pay their foster carers. For some, though, the money is not a primary motivation – payments can be infrequent or stop altogether (I was told of one woman who had received no money for five years).

Angus Geddes, Fostering Development Officer, Swindon Social Services Department, thinks that some private foster mothers would be more than willing to work for the local authority as foster carers if the authority could guarantee them babies to look after.

As AFAS (1997) notes, mature women who have raised their own children and who are well established locally could offer good care for the children of other people, and, indeed, might make excellent recruits to the local authority foster care service (some authorities have recruited them). But a majority of the social workers and health visitors to whom AFAS spoke did not find this to be the case. The study was told:

> Some of these foster parents, from the way they bring up their own children, seem to have a very limited view of parenthood, and don't seem to go beyond seeing it as providing shelter, food and clothing … I think in a number of cases they have simply opted out, beyond these three basic areas.

And:

> A lot of [private foster carers' own children] have had involvement [previously] with social services … non-attendance at school, problems at school, slipping into offending outside school … much of that being attributable perhaps to shortcomings in parenting. Hence the raised eyebrows when one finds these are the families who are doing the private fostering of Nigerian children.

AFAS also collated the responses to private foster carers by 42 social workers, a majority of whom had recent experience of dealing with private foster carers. They stated their characteristics as being:

● *Reluctance … to work with [social worker] to carry out statutory responsibilities*

● *Difficulties: abuse, threats, slander, lack of co-operation*

● *Children extremely well cared for; usually foster carers insist on family contact …*

The carer was paid £10 a week [1997] and supplied everything … but was told that if she

LUCY

It was a health visitor who brought four-year-old Lucy to the attention of a Midlands social services department. She was being privately fostered by the family's next door neighbour, Jane, a single woman of 30 without children of her own, whose mother, Pat, also lived in the house. She had been 'in and out of the house' since birth. Jane's looking after Lucy had started as baby sitting and, as the social worker said, 'had grown and grown'. Lucy's mother, Kate, who was the same age as Jane, was a single mother with three other children. When Lucy's "first family", as the social worker significantly termed it, moved away, they left Lucy with Jane and Pat.

The social services department had questions about how much Lucy could understand of the arrangement and how much she knew of her own birth family background. The physical standards in the foster home were 'just good enough' and while there was not much stimulation, there was more than Lucy was likely to experience with Kate. It was, said the social worker, 'adoption by the backdoor – literally'. Lucy remains in the care of her private foster mother.

Then there is the carer who sees black babies as "toys", or who gains some status from being seen to look after children, or who is compensating for her unsatisfactory raising of her own children, or whose own children have been taken into care.

made a fuss he [the child's birth father] would remove the child [aged 15] even though the child had been with the carer since she was very young.

The white carers' lack of knowledge or understanding about the needs of black children and ... reluctant to enter into discussions about these ... the carers have patronising attitudes towards black children ... and regard them as some sort of "novelty" to which they can give "new" British names because the children's real names are [too] difficult to pronounce.

Then there is the carer who sees black babies as "toys", or who gains some status from being seen to look after children, or who is compensating for her unsatisfactory raising of her own children, or whose own children have been taken into care – such a private foster mother will not see what she is entering into as the simple provision of a service, yet this is what the parent believes is being offered.

However, one private foster carer to whom I spoke said she would never do it again. She is white and lives with her black female partner. They have adopted children and care for a black British boy, Robert, as they did once for his sister Jessica (see page 23). Patricia told me: 'Private fostering is something I would never do again, and if anyone asked me if they should, I would say no unless it was very clear what the parents' expectations are and that the child knows what is going on. Everyone – the carers, the birth parents and the children – are very, very vulnerable in these situations and more safeguards need to be in place.

'We simply and naively got involved because we gave Robert and Jessica an unconditional love

'Private fostering is something I would never do again, and if anyone asked me if they should, I would say no unless it was very clear what the parents' expectations are and that the child knows what is going on.'

that seemed to have nothing to do with the processes of the law. But the Climbié case seemed the worst possible example of what can happen when parents entrust their child to the "care" of others. Robert and Jessica's parents left them with us, strangers, whom they knew nothing about. I have been to Nigeria and the culture and attitudes to child rearing are so different. I have puzzled about it and been fascinated about it for years but the Climbié case seemed to lance a boil.'

The 1997 AFAS study also highlighted networks of carers which often meant that the children were moved around not just in the local area but over some geographical distance, most of them, of course, being anyway initially placed some distance from their parents. AFAS did say that this was difficult to validate but said that it had 'considerable circumstantial evidence to support it'. One person to whom I spoke said that she rang a telephone number pretending to want private foster care and was asked where she would like the child to go – the respondent could arrange placements anywhere in the country.

5 Who are the children?

While the most we know about the numbers of privately fostered children or the numbers who care for them are, at best, educated guesses, we do know who some of the children are, even if, in most cases, we know very little about them.

The largest group of children who are privately fostered are West African (mainly Nigerian) children.

Despite a century and a quarter of legislation on private fostering, it is only in the last 30 years, much of it thanks to Holman's pioneering work, that the subject has insinuated itself into professional consciousness but then only spasmodically. One suspects that, like child abuse, it is a subject that has always been in the public consciousness because it has always been a part of local knowledge or lore. There are several historical references to what we would call private fostering which date it back to Celtic and Nordic people with more formal forms emerging in 11th- and 12th-century Germany (see Triseliotis, Sellick and Short, 1995; and Boswell, 1991). Wet-nursing in 19th-century Britain is much better known.

The largest group of children who are privately fostered are West African (mainly Nigerian) children. Then there are children attending language schools; pupils in independent boarding schools who live away from parents in the school holidays; the children of parents working unsociable hours, which has tended to be identified as the Chinese community; backdoor, pre-adoption arrangements, often from overseas; children arriving as part of a cultural exchange; and those coming into the country because of a national disaster like Chernobyl. Holman (1973) adds the children of single mothers and those whose mothers have been deserted by their

MARTHA

Martha came from Nigeria as a student and met and married another Nigerian student, Kofi, in South Shields. When their first child was born they were living in student accommodation and approached the social services department for help. It advised them to make their own arrangements for child care. They did and found Angela, a private foster carer who was also a registered foster mother. Angela assured the couple that she would never keep their baby or apply to adopt him and the baby was placed with her for three months. Every Friday, Martha would travel to the southern county where her baby lived and stay with the foster mother, returning to South Shields on Monday.

When Martha and Kofi had their second child, the fostering arrangements were so satisfactory that the new baby joined his brother in the foster mother's care. Soon after the baby's birth, Kofi, his studies complete, returned to Nigeria where he had the prospect of a good job.

When Martha had finished her studies in South Shields, she decided to further her education in London. Her plan would be then to get a job and have her children living with her. But until then she continued to spend weekends with her sons at the foster mother's home. When Martha suggested to Angela that she was thinking about her sons coming to live with her, Angela would suggest that she should continue with her studies and Angela would continue to look after the children.

Martha then found a job and a flat and regularised her immigration status. The boys were still in the care of their foster mother but were accustomed to visiting their mother in her new home. But then came the occasion when Martha went to see her children, came back to London and a few days later was served with an ex parte interim residence order in Angela's favour. This was in defiance of the usual practice of an application being served with seven days' notice allowed before the hearing. Angela had stated that Martha had abandoned her children and physically abused them and planned to spirit them off to Africa – even though they were Nigerian citizens. Martha had been unaware that any proceedings were being undertaken.

Confronted by Martha, Angela claimed that a social worker had advised her to apply for the order, although there had been no social work intervention. However, when Martha contacted social services they told her that she had abandoned her children. Angela had never told social services that Martha had had frequent contact with her children and had even stayed at her home at weekends. The children, now five and eight, became frightened of their mother and even threatened to kill themselves.

At a hearing on the order, Angela agreed that the boys would eventually be returned to Martha but that each year she had persuaded Martha to finish her studies and not take the children back.

All expert witnesses – with the exception of two white ones – advised that the children should be returned to their mother. The official solicitor was of the same opinion. The Judge condemned Martha as incoherent (she spoke with a Nigerian accent) and said she was a liar. However, reluctantly, he granted her a residence order. But when Angela refused to return the boys, adding further allegations against Martha, the judge refused two applications to enforce his own order. Angela went on television programmes and was interviewed by newspapers where she claimed that Martha intended to "kidnap" her sons.

Eventually the court made a residence order in favour of Angela on the grounds that the children – now seven and ten – were more attached to her than to Martha. Martha was given limited contact, which is now sporadic and at the whim of Angela.

The boys perceive themselves as "white", they are the only black children in their school and they call themselves by Angela's surname.

Kofi used to make periodic visits from Nigeria to visit his wife and children. The British High Commission in Lagos will now no longer grant him a visa to enter the UK.

fathers, though other writers mention neither group and they probably fall into some of the other categories. Another group infrequently mentioned are children whose parents move house but arrange for their children to live away from home in order to finish their education or complete school examinations (Woollard and

Clarke in Wheal, 1999). Several people to whom I spoke said that they commonly came across a group who are also cited rarely in the literature – young people (often young women) who are in conflict with their parents and move in with a boyfriend and his parents or to the home of a friend.

Children of West African parents

AFAS (quoted Woollard, 1991) reckoned that 80–90 per cent of placements involved West African (mainly Nigerian) children. There is no way of supporting or challenging that percentage at the moment but, undoubtedly, those children do make up a large part, and are possibly a majority, of privately fostered children. They were also at one time very publicly advertised as children available to private foster carers in the columns of *Nursery World*. (Advertising, which began in 1955, only came to an end in 1996 in the wake of a television exposé of private fostering.) Holman (1973) said that 60.8 per cent of privately fostered children were West Africans and the majority of them were from Nigeria.

The overwhelming majority of West African children are placed with white families, raising problems of racism, the child's separation from his or her culture, and of the child's own sense of identity.

The placement of these children also poses a unique problem – they are, of course, subject, as is any privately fostered child, to the possibility of abuse and to be cared for in poor conditions. But that the overwhelming majority of these children are placed with white families (a much higher proportion than of black children placed transracially by local authorities with registered carers or adopted transracially), raises problems of racism, the child's separation from his or her culture, and of the child's own sense of identity.

Private fostering is never unproblematic and any long-term arrangement (as opposed to, say, those for language students or young people who live, usually temporarily, with a friend's family because of a domestic conflict) has the effect of hindering the bonding between parent and child. One black social worker told me that she had been privately fostered, with her sibling, as a child. It was a very positive experience in many ways, she said, so much so that she kept in contact with her foster mother until the latter's death earlier this year. But it was an experience that not merely distanced her from her parents – there were times when the two children did not see their parents – but when they came to visit, she said she didn't like them: her home was not with them, her home was with her foster mother.

The problematic nature of much private fostering (effectively, that of West African children) is partly due to the fact that parent and carer can enter into the arrangement from very different and complex perspectives.

The private fostering of West African children dates back to the 1950s. Then many young couples, coming to this country, separated by continents from their wider family and communal networks, and living in unsatisfactory conditions while attempting to combine work and study, found private foster care their only child care option.

There is a common perception that West African parents believe that allowing their children to live with white English people will give the child a good upbringing with a good command of the language. They also believe that their children will get a good education if living in a white rural area (Atkinson and Horner, 1990). As Theresa Shyanbola, Manager of the African Women's Welfare Association, puts it: 'They want their children to end up half English and half African and be proud of it.'

But the irony of the emphasis on education, Iris Amoah, Team Manager, London Borough of Newham points out, is that many of the foster carers do not give a high priority to education.

One person who took part in the 1993 inspection visited private foster carers and their child. She told me:

'In some places, unless a child was tall enough to see in a mirror, it would never see a black face.'

I asked them if they had any ethnically sensitive toys and they took from behind the settee a brand-new golliwog. The little girl took one look at it and ran to the other side of the room – she was pinned against the wall. The foster carers turned to me and said: 'It's strange but she doesn't seem to like it.' When I heard that and looked at the child up against the wall on the other side of the room, I realised the meaning of the phrase about having no-one to turn to.

She also remembers asking a couple if they knew the religion of the child for whom they were caring. They argued about it – the woman claiming that the child was a Muslim and the man saying that she was a Christian 'because of the holy water they gave us'.

When she met private foster carers as a group, she found that they were well-intentioned but few had any idea of the cultural needs of the children in their care. 'In some places,' she said, 'unless a child was tall enough to see in a mirror, it would never see a black face.'

Beverley Clarke, Health Visitor and Chairperson of the Private Fostering Special Interest Group of the Community Practitioners and Health Visitors Association, first became aware of private fostering ten years ago when a child she visited broke his arm when being swung by two other children in the family. She discovered that the child was being privately fostered. Her awareness was also raised when she and colleagues noticed that sometimes they would see a baby for their check-up immediately after birth but the baby would not be available for the six-week check. Then they would receive a call from a health visitor in, say, Portsmouth asking for details about the baby who was now living there but with someone other than its mother. Then the child might reappear at the clinic or family home a few years later.

In 1990, Beverley Clarke carried out a small study among health visitors in west Lambeth (in Clarke, 1999). A hundred children were identified as being privately fostered but this did not include children aged five and above. The study revealed a variety of problems: behavioural problems (17 per cent), speech and language delay (16 per cent), developmental delays (10 per cent). Seven per cent of the children looked at by Clarke were identified as suffering physical or emotional abuse and neglect and four per cent had suffered sexual abuse. The remaining 44 per cent studied by her were assumed to be developing normally.

Utting (1997) said that privately fostered children appear to be more vulnerable to abuse and neglect than children in local authority foster

A child now aged 15, attends special school after being passed from one carer to the next. His mother said that private fostering was the worst thing she had ever done.

A young girl returned to her family in London, never having seen a black person and so alienated from her background that at the sight of black people she would run away. She said that if she had a dog she would never foster it.

A girl of 16 has been so traumatised by being privately fostered that she will not sleep over at friends' houses, while a boy of 16 wets his bed. He was only privately fostered for a year at three but constantly asks his mother: 'Why did you leave me?'

care, and said: '… indeed, an unknown number are likely to be seriously at risk'. *Signposts*, the report of the 1993 Social Services Inspectorate inspections, referred to 'very real concerns about the welfare of the children'. (Department of Health, 1994). More evidence for this comes from the AFAS report (1991). This reported that in one county there were several cases of abuse (two of them sexual abuse) which warranted legal action. Thirteen social services departments also told AFAS that they had taken children into care after removing them from private foster homes. Afolabi (1990) reports that in another area, an 18-month-old was killed when falling downstairs because there was no stair gate in use and the carer poorly supervised the child.

The health of all children should be protected but there have been cases where children's health has suffered because the carers did not have their medical records. But special problems arise where health issues peculiar to one group of children are unknown to their carers because they are unaware of matters arising from the child's different racial or cultural background. Nesbitt (1990), in a study of African children and their families, showed that the takeup of development surveillance of under-fives was low; 12 per cent of the children had language problems; and 10 per cent of mothers screened in 1988 for Hepatitis B were carriers. Sickle cell disorders affect mainly Africans and African-Caribbeans but also people of Mediterranean, Asian and Arabic origin. And while white foster carers may be ignorant of this, Nesbitt's research showed that only 10 per cent of the birth mothers were aware of their child's sickle cell status. It would be very easy for this to go unnoticed in private foster care with potentially fatal results.

They had been made to lick up urine, the "carers" had stood on their throats and they had had cigarettes put out in their faces.

LOLA

Lola was seven years old when she was placed by arrangement through a third party. Josie Wright, her carer, had no information about Lola's parents other than what the person who arranged the placement told her. When the health visitor called to do a visit, having been told of the arrangement by the local health department, the child had gone; indeed, there was no evidence that she had ever been in the household. Two years later a neighbour reported concerns about Lola and the same health visitor undertook a visit to discover that the child had been locked away for two years because Josie Wright, lacking information, had been unable to contact the parents.

Lola lacked health and dental care and had never been to school. She was so thin that the health visitor could put her fingers around her wrist. She was removed from the house and is now living happily with her mother in Nigeria. However, her mother had never known that her daughter was even in the UK; she had thought she was elsewhere in Europe with her father.

Parents also seem not to know that private fostering can involve brokering – this is where private foster mothers take a child and then pass the child onto someone else. In one case, in south London, a mother, wanting to enquire about her baby, could not reach the carer with whom she had placed the child and eventually found that she was with someone else.

Another mother only discovered where her third child was living when the second carer called her because she happened to discover her address from the baby's medical card, which she had been given. She had had the child for two weeks, she said, because he had been distressed with the first carer. The child returned to the mother in a distressed and disturbed state.

How easily private foster carers can come by other people's children is illustrated by Jackie Oldfield, Service Manager, Havant & Petersfield, Hampshire County Council. She tells of an incident when she was a social worker and was visiting a client. The visit was interrupted by a neighbour coming in, carrying a baby and exclaiming: 'Look what I've got! My friend had her for a week but she doesn't want her anymore.'

When Yewande and Taiwo Ogunnaike were interviewed on *Black Bag* (1997), they wanted to know why they had been placed, as toddlers, in private foster care. Their two brothers had then joined them. They had been made to lick up urine, the "carers" had stood on their throats and they had had cigarettes put out in their faces. Neighbours had complained to social services and all the children had been taken into care but there had been no prosecution. On those occasions when they had met their mother, they were alienated from her: 'Who is this woman?' they said they would ask. No-one – their parents or their foster carers – had been made accountable for their care. When, in later life, they asked their father, he could only say: 'I am sorry. Please forgive me.'

The Olympic runner Kriss Akabusi and his brother, Riba, were also abused in private care – at a placement in King's Cross they were made to drink urine. They, too, told *Black Bag* that they became detached from their parents. 'What was a mum?' said Riba when he learned that his mother was to visit from Nigeria. They had no direct route back into Nigerian culture. Riba went to Africa when he was 20 but was seen as, in his words, 'an English boy in a black skin', even to his sister and his father.

Of their mother, Kriss Akabusi said:

The reality was she came to England to find her boys and we weren't there, we were different people. We were not her ideal Nigerian boys. Unfortunately, my mother died having lost everything.

'Children always come back to their roots – everyone does; we know it through adoption – but these children, when they do, often return to parents who have to deal with a disturbed child.'

'Children', believes Joy Okoye, a barrister, who has been involved in cases about private

GRACE

Ronald and Julie Havers were an English couple running a children's home in South Africa. Grace was a toddler who had two sisters and a brother, all older than her, and they were all living with their extended family. The children's mother was an alcoholic and nothing was known about their father. The Havers had taken Grace to the UK for a holiday and wanted to take her there to live permanently. But when her mother died, her grandmother began to take an interest in the youngest grandchild. However, Grace was allowed to come to the UK with the Havers as a privately fostered child. Although the Havers' marriage broke up, Julie sought to adopt Grace, who was living with her in Wales in an area where there were no other black people. Her grandmother came to London to be represented at the adoption hearing. When Grace was two-and-a-half, the adoption was allowed. Grace has been visited by her sisters, brother, great-uncle and grandmother.

HENRY

Henry, the child of Nigerian parents, was just a year old when he was placed with Doreen, a white, childless single woman. His mother was killed in a road accident and his father returned to Africa when Henry was five. Doreen received her payments regularly when Henry's father was living in the UK but when he returned home they became sporadic.

When Henry was seven, his father wrote to Doreen to ask her to return his son to Nigeria where he could live with his aunt. Doreen replied that she wanted to keep Henry – it didn't matter about the money. This was agreed and Henry had some contact with his father and aunts until he was 11.

Then an invitation came for Henry to go and spend the summer holidays with his father and his family. Doreen told Henry that he didn't want to go and spend time with 'those blacks'. Henry was horrified at the prospect. He didn't want to go. He said he 'belonged in England'. He and Doreen wrote to refuse the invitation.

Henry is now one of only three black children at his secondary school. He is often in trouble with teachers and is known to the police for shoplifting. One of his teachers has talked to a social worker, a friend, about the 'strange home situation' in which Henry finds himself but there has been no action on the part of the local authority.

Since Henry told his father he did not want to go on holiday there has been no contact.

fostering, 'always come back to their roots – everyone does; we know it through adoption. But these children, when they do, often return to parents who have to deal with a disturbed child.'

Okoye has dealt with a number of cases where West African parents have contested adoption and residence orders applied for with regard to their children. In Africa, she explains, children are raised more communally, relying on extended family, friends and neighbourhood. Such carers are often found or recommended by word of mouth in a culture that is an oral one. Okoye quotes the African proverb – 'It takes a village to raise a child' – to explain arrangements which sit in sharp contrast to Western (and certainly British) reliance on the nuclear family as the primary way by which children are cared for.

She would never advise West African parents to use white private foster carers unless the latter gave an undertaking that the arrangement would be temporary and that they had no intention of seeking to adopt the children or to apply for a residence order.

Iris Amoah says:

> The mistake too many parents make is transplanting the structures from where they come from to here, without thinking through the racism and also, of course, there is their own internalised racism – if people are white, they must be good. Nor do they take into account the implications of their decisions for their children. Parents make these decisions looking at their circumstances just as anyone would and they see that childminding doesn't suit them and they don't want their children moved around. Looked at like that, private fostering seems a reasonable option.

For Joy Okoye, the possibility of parents losing their children to their foster carers stems from the prejudice against black parents on the part of the judiciary – judges see private fostering arrangements as evidence of negligent parenting.

ROBERT AND JESSICA

Patricia and Adjua were a same-sex couple, living in London, when, 13 years ago, they decided to help out Victoria, a Nigerian, with Robert, her new born baby son. Victoria had wanted Adjua's cousin, a childminder, to look after the boy and when she said she could not, threatened to leave him on her doorstep.

'We were naïve,' Adjua now admits. 'We really didn't know what we were doing or how long we would be looking after Robert for. We didn't know why Victoria wanted us to do this – were she and her husband poor? Did they want to have children without the responsibility of looking after them? These were questions we didn't ask, or worry too much when we didn't get the answers.'

But they did look after Robert and when his sister, Jessica, was born a year later she, too, came into their care but not before Victoria said the alternative would be that she would have to send Jessica to Nigeria. Jessica, like her brother, was four months old when she went to live with Patricia and Adjua. (Victoria has another son, now aged 19, by a previous relationship. He has always lived with her and Philip.) It was not an obviously problematic arrangement at the beginning. Victoria and her husband, Philip, also lived in London and every three weeks they would see their children.

Patricia and Adjua eventually moved house and went a good way from the capital and over the years adopted four children – their twins are now 12 and came to them when they were seven. Their other two children, now five and two, were adopted when they were both a year old.

Occasionally, Victoria would talk about her children returning to her but they continued to live with Patricia and Adjua. But until then, the children were brought to London to see their parents and,

infrequently, the parents would travel to see them. Victoria's wish for Robert's return rather than Jessica's seemed to be because he was approaching school age. But Patricia and Adjua could see confusion building in the children's minds, and the attachment which they had formed to them. As they prepared Robert for his entry into a local school, they feared disruption if his mother demanded he return to live in London only days before he was due to start. They also knew how close the children were to one another. They would also have to fit back into the very different life of their birth parents.

Victoria's attitude was to tell Patricia and Adjua: 'Look at it as if Robert is going to boarding school but he will stay with you in the school holidays.'

And so eventually, both Robert, six, and Jessica, five, went back to London. But Patricia and Adjua would come to visit them and every holiday, except Christmas, the children would stay with them.

As a harbinger of things to come, Robert often said to his foster carers: 'I know if I had the choice, I would come to live with you. This family just doesn't suit me.'

It may be that, as the years went by, Victoria came to feel that she had done something with her children which she deeply regretted but which had set in train consequences which neither she nor anyone else could now undo.

A year ago, Victoria told Patricia and Adjua that the children would no longer be coming to stay in the holidays and that if they wanted to see them, they could do so in their home in London. They did see them, just before Christmas. It was tense and Victoria accused Patricia and Adjua of giving Robert £20 without her permission (in fact, they were passing on a present from another friend). It gave Victoria the excuse she needed: Patricia and Adjua, she said, could no longer see or telephone the children any more.

Robert's distress at this was shown when he returned to school and started to 'phone Patricia and Adjua. He wanted, he said, to 'divorce' his parents and live with them. His threat to run away was not idle. One day, instead of going to school, he caught the train to their home.

In order to gain breathing space, Patricia and Adjua successfully applied for a Prohibited Steps Order and Victoria agreed in court that she would hand over Robert's medical card, passport and the Child Benefit book. Robert told Patricia and Adjua that she would not; they disagreed. Victoria never did.

In a counter move, Victoria and Philip applied for a residence order and requested that Robert be placed in a registered foster home until the case was settled. Patricia and Adjua also sought a residence order for Robert. The court asked for an independent social work assessment. The residence order was granted. No contact order was made but Patricia and Adjua are hoping that, at a later hearing, one should be made. They argue that, even if Robert has no wish ever to see his parents again and will not see his sister, whom he does very much want to see, at their house, Victoria and Philip should not be made to feel that their relationship with their son, whom they do want to see, is over.

Today Robert has gained entry to a highly regarded school of music. He says: 'I don't know why my parents did what they did. People don't do that to kids. How can someone say that they love you and make you go through that? It makes you messed up. I don't want to see them. I don't know them very well. Patricia and Adjua are my parents. I now have to get on with things in my life.' He says he now feels some security with the residence order 'as before my parents could have come and got me'.

In June this year he wrote a letter to his mother saying that she had treated him 'like dirt', and that he was never coming back. He accused her of manipulating his sister's feelings by having her feel that she could not love her parents and love Patricia and Adjua. He ended the letter: 'What is all this about parental love? Love is something that happens when you care for someone; it has nothing to do with blood.'

Jessica is now caught in the middle and is refusing to have any contact with Patricia, Adjua, their adopted children or her brother, Robert.

Patricia says that she and Adjua would not consider adopting Robert because his parents want him and the parents of their adoptive children are either dead or unable to care for them.

She said: 'Private fostering is something I would never do again and if anyone asked me if they should, I would say no, unless it was very clear what the parents' expectations are and that the child knows what is going on. Everyone – the carers, the birth parents and the children – are very, very vulnerable in these situations and more safeguards need to be in place.

'Obviously we have told this story on the basis of how we – Adjua, Robert and myself – experienced these events. It is likely that Victoria and Philip see it differently.'

The curious appendix to this story is that in all the years that Robert and his sister lived with Patricia and Adjua, no-one ever informed them that they were legally obliged to inform the local authority of the arrangement. The children went to school, health visitors called, Jessica went into hospital a couple of times for asthma. And Patricia and Adjua had frequent contact with the social services department when they adopted their other children.

Eighty-five per cent of the cases with which Joy Okoye has dealt or of which she knows through colleagues have had judgements favourable to the foster carers. When a case comes up, she says that she and colleagues invariably say, 'you may as well forget it' so slim are the chances of their client winning.

Joy Okoye adds:

The law has a rationale, but those who implement it do not and so much depends on the individual judge. Race is – as Oscar Wilde said of his homosexuality – like the love that dare not speak its name. You can now talk openly about sexuality but you can't about race. I raise matters of race in court when appropriate, when relevant, never in a spurious way. But when I do, there is a frisson but that is not my intention and it should not be. But once the issue is raised then it marks you out as a hostile person. The difficulty is that most judges have the view that they are not prejudiced but they are not prepared to accept the concept of equality in diversity. But when you can do that, you can make appropriate decisions for children. Judges would rather avoid that debate – it is dismissed as anecdotal.

Iris Amoah says:

The best parents always lose their children because they are too transparent – they tell the foster carer everything. The happiness of their children is what the parents want and the closer the child's relationship is to the foster carer, the happier it will be – and that's what the problem is: it's more likely that that kind of carer will go for a residence order.

She tells of a private foster mother taking out proceedings to keep the child, and her mother having to kidnap the child and go into hiding before returning to Nigeria.

The detachment of children from their parents so that they come to identify with the carer is

Given that the foster carers are white, the detachment of the child from the parents is also a detachment from his or her heritage and cultural and racial identity.

another reason why the courts look favourably on residence orders and adoption applications – the children's interests are seen as best served by them staying where they are. Holman (1973) found that 41 per cent of carers did not talk to the children about why they were in their care, and many of the carers had given no indication of how long the placement would last. Fifty per cent of foster carers, he reported, practised "exclusive" fostering – they treated the children as their own and they did not treat the parents as partners. This created obvious problems for the child to understand their identity and when he or she was to return to the birth parents. Today the same situation prevails. As Peter Fry, Director of International Social Service, puts it: 'Our experience is that time takes over and determines decisions.'

Given that the foster carers are white, the detachment of the child from the parents is also a detachment from his or her heritage and cultural and racial identity. Lack of awareness of these issues is common among foster carers, even where they are not openly racist. In 1991, the African Family Advisory Service said that some racist private foster carers would threaten children with being returned to Africa and reported on terms some carers would use like "darkie", "blackie" and "nigger".

An extreme and extremely damaging example of racism is that of the four-year-old black boy who was always told, after he had washed his hands, that there was no way of knowing if they were clean. By six he had become an "obsessional washer", which affected his education and physical and mental health and led to him needing therapy (Maximé, 1993).

AFAS (1997) found examples of racial abuse and insensitivity: a Nigerian child told that he was "white underneath" when he cut himself; a social worker who witnessed racial abuse of the fostered child by the carer's children which she did not stop; and those who said that they were "colour blind" and saw no need to keep the children in touch with their culture and languages or seek opportunities for them to meet others of the same ethnic group.

There is no way, at present, of measuring the extent of such abuse. Several people to whom I spoke could remember their own local authorities taking into care children who were privately fostered. As a result of the 1996 programme on private fostering, in the television series *Black Britain*, which looked only at Shropshire, Staffordshire and Warwickshire, four children under the age of ten went into care. (This programme also unveiled widespread networks of white families fostering black children, and also led to the decision of *Nursery World* no longer to take advertisements seeking foster carers.)

There are other ways, too, in which parents can lose their children. Theresa Shyanbola, Manager of the African Women's Welfare Association, says

BUCHI AND HER SISTER

Femi and Amma were Nigerians living in a London borough. He was a law student and she was working. When they became parents of a baby girl, Buchi, Amma found that a workmate knew Sandra, a British woman who was a private foster carer, living only a few streets from them. Sandra took on the baby's care and when a second child was born, she, too, went to Sandra. Until Sandra moved to another borough, Femi and Amma were seeing their daughters almost every day, often casually calling in. And even when Sandra moved, the parents would frequently see the children, especially at weekends.

It appeared to be a satisfactory relationship and the children were in Sandra's care for seven years. But, without informing Femi and Amma, Sandra successfully applied for a residence order. The children developed an antipathy towards anything Nigerian and Sandra had made negative remarks about their mother's accent. The parents' case had been undermined by Sandra's local social services department which had reported positively when they visited the placement and had found that the children attended school and mixed well and that they lived in a multiracial area.

Femi and Amma's marriage broke up under the strain and both their daughters were seeing a therapist in their teens.

In 1991, the African Family Advisory Service said that some racist private foster carers would threaten children with being returned to Africa and reported on terms some carers would use like "darkie", "blackie" and "nigger".

that she is personally aware of ten children having gone missing in the last five years – parents, their friends or relatives go to visit the children and the family is no longer living at the address. In one case, in Dover, an adolescent brother and sister had been in private foster care since 1990 and their aunt arrived to find the house no longer standing. It had been demolished as part of a redevelopment scheme. This would appear to bear out Utting's claim that some children "disappear" (Utting, 1997).

The long-term effects for black children who are privately fostered can be a confusion about their identity, problems in relationships, difficulty in demonstrating love, labelling, under-achievement at school, insecurity, mental ill health, poor speech development, social and behavioural and learning difficulties, misdiagnosis, and flashbacks (Clarke, 1999). Any child could be subject to these but they affect black children particularly because they are the one group of children who are privately fostered who we know spend sometimes years in the care of people not their parents.

One real problem in understanding how extensive these adverse experiences are is that, although individual practitioners will know of cases and some are described in the literature, there is no quantitative research. Also, the way that services operate militates against the development of knowledge. Generally speaking, children from minority ethnic groups are under-represented in specialist child mental health settings unless services make very specific and careful provision to make their services accessible to these families. The charity, Young Minds, was not aware of any projects working with West African families when asked.

It is also the case that children who live in alternative family placements are also under-represented in these settings and those who are referred to them tend to be children in the care of local authorities. But when it comes to mental health services for adults, there is an over-representation of people from minority ethnic communities. While seeking the reasons for this is not the purpose of this report, there must be at least a prima facie case to consider whether this over-representation is, in some part, due to the experience of being privately fostered transracially when children.

As Beverley Clarke said:

> It is almost as if these children do not count. The tragedy is that they look to their parents and society to make life bearable for them and yet we fail them and at what cost?

The long-term effects for black children who are privately fostered can be a confusion about their identity, problems in relationships, difficulty in demonstrating love, labelling, under-achievement at school, insecurity, mental ill health, poor speech development, social and behavioural and learning difficulties, misdiagnosis, and flashbacks.

Overseas students

Some people have claimed to me that children who attend language schools may be moved from one placement to another to avoid meeting the criteria of the 28-day rule. If questioned, owners of the schools can then say that they are observing the law or, at least, are not required to notify the local authority. However, it was clearly not the intention of the Children Act 1989 that the welfare safeguards could be circumvented by moving a child every 27 days.

There are no reliable figures about the numbers of schools because they do not have to be registered or about the numbers of pupils who come to them. Many schools have been established for many years but anyone can set up such a school. According to McGrath (2001a), one local authority identified a number of language schools with a turnover of more than a thousand children, aged from seven upwards, a year. One school expected to take 5,500 children in a year (Some of whom would not have been privately fostered but there would still be grounds for concern). Another local authority found 35 schools in one resort.

Some years ago, Oxfordshire was taken by surprise when 50 or 60 Russian students came to Oxford as their country started to look outward and barriers to overseas travel came down. They were to stay nine months and the council had very quickly to check all the accommodation where they were to stay. But it also did more than that – it produced an information pack for the foster carers and for the young people themselves, and it arranged that information was sent back to Russia to the students' families so that they knew what kind of life the children would be living when away from home. The council also worked with the language schools on how the children could be better looked after – weekend activities, the structure of their days, keeping a check on carers.

Refugee children

Of all the children, the least on which information is available are asylum seekers and Chinese children. Both gain only passing mentions in the literature and those who work in the field know very little about them. For refugee children, the Refugee Council has no knowledge of any private fostering arrangements which may exist. There are no exact figures for asylum seekers entering the country, let alone accompanied children entering the country because only the primary applicant is counted. That person may have two, three or four others (or, of course, none) with him or her. In 1999 there were 71,160 primary applicants and in 2000 there were 76,064. It must be almost certain that the chances are that some children will be privately fostered. Certainly, International Social Service believes this to be the case.

Yet there appears to be no way of finding out what the arrangements are. Attempts to do so are bedevilled by several things, not least the fact that any arrangement for a child to be cared for other

CARL AND ERIC

Carl Williams was 18 months old when Marcia, his mother, placed him with Audrey Simmons, a family friend and fellow Jamaican. It was believed that Marcia Williams was deported to Jamaica for drug offences. Carl's father, Edmund Collins, who was not married to his mother, was believed to be living in London. Eric Francis was also 18 months when he joined Carl in Audrey Simmons' care when Ellen, his mother, was imprisoned, also for drug offences. She, too, was deported upon her release. Eric's father was unknown.

Audrey Simmons had no parental responsibility for either boy and allegations of physical abuse were made. In January this year (2001) Eric said that she hit him with an iron bar and a belt. Medical examinations of both boys showed a number of scars and bruises consistent with their being mistreated. Carl said that Audrey Simmons hit them but denied the assaults which Eric claimed happened. Carl wants to return to live with Audrey; Eric refuses all contact. The boys were placed in the care of the local authority, under an interim care order.

The local authority, using International Social Service, is trying to trace the relatives of both boys in Jamaica. In March a letter, allegedly from Eric's mother, was received saying that Ellen wanted her son to continue to be cared for by Audrey Simmons. There are doubts about the letter's authenticity. Carl's father and Eric's mother have been written to at addresses where they were thought to have been living. No replies were ever received. Carl and Eric remain in local authority care today.

than by a parent or relative will have been made in its native country, which war and conflict may have reduced to administrative, as well as other chaos. How to know or to prove what these arrangements were?

Many children who come to the UK are accompanied by an agent – someone who is paid to bring them – and then are left at airports or somewhere else in the UK. A child is regarded as unaccompanied by the Home Office if he or she is not joining a close relative. Such children then become the responsibility of the host local authority. However, some parents and relatives who make arrangements for children to come in with someone else may believe that that person will be the child's carer after arrival when, in fact, this will not be the case. Or the parent or relative may pretend to themselves, in their desperation to assist their child to flee from the plight at home, that this will be so; the child may actually believe it. Some children may be attached to a group from their home village which is leaving for the UK, some of whom may or may not be related to the child.

But if a child is accompanied, immigration officials have only to satisfy themselves of their immigration status – not the relationship of the accompanying adult to the child. The belief that children will always be travelling with a parent or close relative may be a misapprehension on the part of the immigration authorities.

One private fostering officer told me that though he had written to his own authority's team working with asylum seekers, he had had no response. 'Why don't they see themselves as doing child care?' he asked.

Chinese children

Only marginally more is known about Chinese children than is known about refugee children. One or two people have mentioned to me that private fostering of these children is concentrated in Glasgow. If that were so, there would be no reason to believe that that city was unique and that where there are Chinese communities – in, for example, London and Manchester – practice would not be the same. According to the Race Equality Unit (REU, 1993), Scotland's experience of private fostering is mainly with Chinese children.

Of all the children, the least on which information is available are asylum seekers and Chinese children.

One agency that does know something about this, even if, like most matters appertaining to private fostering, it is frustratingly little, is NCH's San Jai Project in Glasgow. Dorothy Neoh, Project Leader, says that in Glasgow and Edinburgh substitute care is day care. But she does know of private fostering away from Scotland's central region, particularly in Fife and Dumfries and Galloway. This has been going on for well over 20 years, she says, and the problems and patterns here mirror those of West African families. The children are placed with white couples and become alienated from their parents, and there are often problems for the parents in getting the child back. Unfortunately, San Jai is not equipped for work in these remote rural areas away from its main focus, Glasgow.

However, in Oxfordshire, a publicity campaign brought some private fostering of Chinese children to the surface. Plymouth, on the other hand, which has the third largest Cantonese population in the country, has done no work with any group of privately fostered children. Three years ago in Gloucester, Brendan McGrath, Private Fostering Co-ordinator, Gloucestershire County Council, became aware, through a health visitor, of a woman who was privately fostering three Chinese children. She had been involved in this way with this group of children for 20 years. She was English but of Polish descent. Her husband was in employment and their own children had left home. (The Chinese in Gloucester are from two groups: those who speak Hakke and Cantonese and have a poor command of English, and long-standing residents whose English is good.)

The REU (1993) claimed that the placements were transracial and San Jai says this is so. In Oxfordshire, at least, it is believed that Chinese children, unlike most West African children, are privately fostered locally, and, thus, even if transracially placed, have more contact with their parents (and thus their culture) than many West African children or Chinese children from Scotland's more rural areas. The REU said that the children 'will probably spend some part of the week in their own family'. Woollard and Clarke (in Wheal, 2000) say that there are 'significant' numbers of Chinese children privately fostered but they, too, adduce no evidence to support the claim. The REU report makes the point that the child care needs of people who work unsocial hours fall outside the usual provision made by social services or the private sector.

Children on holiday, exchange visits and at independent schools

Children from Chernobyl, where the nuclear power station explosion took place in April 1986, are only the most public and saddest of all those children who come to the UK each year through sponsored holiday visits or as part of exchanges. Children from Northern Ireland are another group who have come to mainland Britain as a result of dramatic circumstances in their own country, partly through the work of the Corremeela community. There are 135 Chernobyl Life Line Links in this country and since 1992, over 16,500 children from Chernobyl have spent a month or more here and continue to come each year.

For the parents of some children who attend independent schools, especially those who live overseas, whether British expatriates or citizens of their countries, there is the guardianship organisation. These are private companies. Their job is to recruit host families for such children. They cannot, of course, carry out the kind of checks which would fall to a local authority but they are able, if they wish, to liaise with the local authorities for the areas where their children live (see Chapter 6, *Someone to turn to?*).

Children in other situations

There are three other groups of children who end up in private foster care about whom little is known, not least how many there are.

The first group are those who arrive with diplomats and who may end up as domestic slaves and be sexually and physically abused. Heloise Kareem, Case Worker with International Social Service, says that the organisation is aware, through the cases which come its way – perhaps two or three a year – of 'a steady trickle' of children who are brought in from abroad by diplomats, from African and Arab states, to work as unpaid domestic help. Because diplomats are allowed to be accompanied by others whom they say are dependent relatives, immigration checks are not made on them.

The second group of children are those whose parents are sent to prison or, if from overseas, deported. In the case of deported parents, once in their home country efforts to trace them may be unavailing.

The last group of children are back door, pre-adoptive placements, often from overseas where the prospective parents have not given notification to adopt and such a child cannot be a "protected child" under adoption law. This group of children attracted much attention only this year when the Kilshaws arrived in the UK from the USA with their so-called "internet twins" but the more controversial aspects of the case overlaid the fact that they were privately fostered.

The last group of children are back door, pre-adoptive placements, often from overseas where the prospective parents have not given notification to adopt and such a child cannot be a "protected child" under adoption law.

Refugee and Chinese children, the pathetic domestic slaves, the children of imprisoned or deported parents, and the children of back door adoptions – these are other, albeit the most dramatic puzzles, wrapped in the enigma that envelops private fostering like low-lying cloud.

ANNE-MARIE

Anne-Marie had been sleeping for two nights in a small north London park when she was spotted early one morning three years ago sitting on a low wall in a nearby street by Kate Mulvey. She went across to speak to her. The girl was dirty and wearing clothes and shoes that did not fit her; later, when she took off the shoes, her feet were bleeding. She could speak only French. Kate Mulvey called at the house of her friend and neighbour Claire Johnson as she knew that she could speak French. When she approached her, the girl was reluctant to say anything other than that she came from the Ivory Coast. But with the friendly overtures and being taken to Claire's house where she was fed, given new clothes and was able to have a bath, her story emerged.

She said that she was 12 but it seemed likely that she was younger. About six or seven months earlier a couple had called to see the woman believed to be her grandmother (she may have been her mother) in the village where they lived in the Ivory Coast. The couple, said her grandmother, were long-lost relatives who had been living in the city and had come to make contact with their extended family. They were a professional couple and offered to take Anne-Marie, with their own child, to the UK where she would enjoy a good education. But when in the UK, Anne-Marie was treated as a domestic slave, on call 24 hours a day, doing the housework, having to cook and to take care of the younger child. When what she did was not as the couple wanted she would be beaten, sometimes with kitchen implements. She had rarely left the house and had only once met someone other than the couple and the child. This was a friend of the wife who also came from the Ivory Coast who came to the house. She had heard the woman say: 'You are going too far with that child.'

Anne-Marie had been warned by the couple not to run away 'because you won't get any help from white people' but two days before she was found, the couple had told her to go to the local corner shop. Seeing her chance of escape, she had walked until she came to the park.

Claire Johnson described her as 'like a wild cat. We gave her a bed but she could not sleep.' Asked if she wished to return to the other house, Anne-Marie said: 'No! No!' Kate Mulvey called a friend who was a social worker who advised that the police should be contacted. At 2am the next morning she was taken into the care of the local authority. Today, she has learned some English, goes to school and lives happily with her African-Caribbean local authority foster carer. The social services department have traced her grandmother who is intending to visit.

6 Someone to turn to?

Local authorities are given responsibilities under the Children Act 1989 and earlier legislation to check on the welfare of children in private foster care – supposing, of course, that they know where they are. It is these laws which successive governments have regarded as sufficient and opine that the only problem is that local authorities do not implement them. When the Care Standards Act 2000 was making its way through the Westminster Parliament, ministers resisted attempts to have private fostering included in the regime of inspections by the Care Standards Commission.

The second claim by Government – that local authorities do not carry out the statutory legislative responsibilities which they have – is correct insofar as most councils are concerned. Almost all local authorities give very low priority to private fostering. In one authority, it was believed that policies and practice were in place. But a recent inspection by the Social Services Inspectorate found there were fine words on paper but no evidence of practice. Several authorities I contacted – including some listed in the ADSS survey (ADSS, 2001) as having officers with a dedicated responsibility – said that policies were just being formulated. One social worker with a specialist responsibility said: 'I have some fieldwork teams that are very co-operative [in bringing placements to his notice] but others that aren't because it just means more work for them.'

There may well be a tendency by some social workers to pretend that the problem does not exist or to give low priority to cases because of pressure on budgets and staff time. Someone in another authority, now working in private fostering, admitted to me that this is what they had done as a team member in the past. One change, which would lessen the dangers of this happening, is if fostering and adoption workers carried out assessments and area teams then provided any social work support needed.

Local authority responsibilities

Sixty-nine per cent of the ADSS's 71 respondents (ADSS, 2001) said that they had a policy on private fostering and 60 per cent of those said that they recorded the number of cases in their areas – which would, of course, be only those cases known to them.

The 1993 official inspection of three authorities (Department of Health, 1994) found services to be sparse and patchy, and accorded a low priority. Some authorities did not have satisfactory arrangements to deal with private fostering; the general public were unaware of the duty of notification; potentially vulnerable children were being placed in families without adequate checks; numbers were unknown; and the arrangements of placements by some parents raised concerns about their children's welfare. A senior civil servant told me that the latest, more extensive inspection, due to be published later this year, would tell much the same story. Not much seems to have been learned between the two inspections and even less to have been done.

Indeed, the ADSS survey itself might stand as an example of the vast majority of local authorities' lack of commitment. First, not much more than a third of social services departments responded (71 out of 179). Second, an analysis of the list of the 18 named as officers said to have a responsibility shows that only a few of the 16 said to have sole responsibility, do, in fact, have this. Third, some of them are difficult to trace due to the authority's name not being given;

The 1993 official inspection of three authorities found services to be sparse and patchy, and accorded a low priority.

one has no name but only a designation – practice co-ordinator – who could not be identified when telephoned. Two names and one address are spelled wrongly; and several of the people named do not have that responsibility any longer (the survey was conducted in February 2001) and in some places it was difficult to discover who had taken it over.

The ignorance of staff about their responsibilities, the law, guidance and regulations has been well documented.

Few of those named do, in fact, have private fostering as their only responsibility and yet only two of the 18 are said to have this responsibility among others. One person, said to have responsibility, laughed when I asked if, in fact, that was the case and said: 'Well, yes – theoretically but I don't know much about it.' Another, asked the same question, said: 'Do you mean independent foster care agencies?' I explained that I did not and said what I meant by private fostering to which the reply was: 'Oh, that kind of fostering. Well, I have some responsibility but I don't know much about it. There's a bit of work done but there's not the volume to justify more.' This kind of remark illustrates the finding of the 1993 inspection of 'a considerable level of confusion and lack of clarity about private fostering' (Department of Health, 1994). Someone in the south west said: 'It is my responsibility but it is also part of a very big Quality Protects agenda.'

The answer to the frequently made argument that services cannot be justified because there is no-one to deliver them is provided by Gloucestershire's Private Fostering Co-ordinator, Brendan McGrath: 'If you look, you find.'

Someone from a voluntary agency told me that she spoke to 15 different people in one local authority, pretending to be a private foster carer wanting to notify, as required by the law. 'Had I not known the ropes I would have given up after I spoke to the first two,' she said, 'and the fact is that none of them knew anything about private fostering.'

The ignorance of staff about their responsibilities, the law, guidance and regulations has been well documented (see African Family Advisory Service, 1997; Department of Health, 1994).

Raising awareness
Twenty-five of the 71 ADSS respondents said that they actively took steps to make people more aware of the need to notify. This was done by advising known cases, displaying leaflets and posters, running advertisements in the local press and placing articles in council newspapers. However, only three social services departments thought that they received notifications as a result of such work. Utting (1997) stated that, where local authorities had attempted publicity campaigns, with posters and local newspaper advertising, they had had very little response. In fact, few of them have done even this.

In June 2000, Denise Platt, Chief Inspector of Social Services, wrote to all directors of social services announcing an inspection of private fostering that would take place in the early part of 2001. She reminded them of their responsibilities and asked that they ensure that their council was complying with legal requirements. She said that ministers had asked the Social Services Inspectorate to run an awareness campaign during 2001 to encourage carers and parents to contact the council in the area where the child was being cared for. The Chief Inspector wanted local authorities to have 'robust' measures in place before the campaign was launched. The effect was a lack of measures, robust or otherwise, and a pamphlet, *Private Fostering: Cause for concern* (Department of Health, 2001) explaining private fostering to professionals, which has been referred to earlier.

While private fostering has not been included until now in the Quality Protects initiative, one local authority wanted it both ways – it included a local voluntary project in its Quality Protects plans as looking after private fostering in its area even though it had never consulted the project about it and overlooked the fact that the project had yet to start work. And even if it had, it would be unable to undertake the statutory duties incumbent upon the local authority.

This is not to say that local authorities are uniformly negligent of their responsibilities but most of them appear to have placed a minimal interpretation on what is already weak legislation. Several have embarked on advertising campaigns without, as I have said, much response. Why this should be we can only guess. But it may well be that some private foster carers do not even see themselves as such – they are 'just looking after someone's child'. Others may fear that the modest sums of money to be made – which may be significant to them given the financial circumstances of many private foster carers – will come to the notice of the taxman. Others may have an exaggerated view of the powers of local authorities. One former registered foster carer, who is now a training officer with a voluntary agency, told me of a neighbour who cared for a child who was obviously not hers. When she enquired, the woman said that she looked after the child while the father, a single parent, was away working on ferries. Advised that she had a duty to notify the local social services department, the woman said: 'I don't want them round here; they will be checking the fireguards and the staircases.' My informant told me that she later noticed that the child was no longer in the woman's care.

Such an example reflects poorly on the nanny state view which many people have of social services, as well as the ignorance which private foster carers may have of just how minimalist are the powers of local authorities in this area, other than in very exceptional circumstances.

An underground activity?

That private foster carers are suspicious of local authorities was highlighted by the REU (1993), when it stated:

> While some parents and carers may actively seek the guidance and support of the local authority, many others will feel suspicious or anxious about involvement with a statutory agency. There is likely to be ignorance of the law and the local authority role.

According to 61 of the 71 respondents to the Association of Directors of Social Services' survey (ADSS, 2001), most private foster carers do not notify because they do not know that they have to; there is no incentive for them to do so (41); they are suspicious of local authorities (35); and they are worried about the child being taken away (16). Widespread ignorance of the duty to notify was also identified by the 1993 inspections (Department of Health, 1994).

AFAS (1997) said that for separate but interlocking reasons, parents and foster carers had developed a 'siege mentality' in their attitudes to staying away from local authorities.

As most private foster carers do not notify, this raises the question of whether registration would be a deterrent to coming forward and

'While some parents and carers may actively seek the guidance and support of the local authority, many others will feel suspicious or anxious about involvement with a statutory agency. There is likely to be ignorance of the law and the local authority role.'

would drive private fostering underground. This mirrors exactly the arguments used when the registration of childminders was introduced more than 30 years ago. Even if they had greater powers, local authorities would need to use them with discretion – a young woman staying with a friend's family is very different from small black children on a run down, all white, out of town housing estate.

As most private foster carers do not notify, this raises the question of whether registration would be a deterrent to coming forward and would drive private fostering underground.

However, the one example I could find of a negligent local authority being brought to book offers some caution in making assumptions about who may or may not need help. In May this year (2001) the local government Commissioner for Local Administration ruled that Lancashire County Council had failed adequately to respond to a complainant's requests for assistance while she was caring for a teenage child who was being privately fostered. The foster carer had asked for a social work assessment and both financial and practical help. The Commissioner, Patricia Thomas, found that the council had failed to comply with its statutory duty to visit her promptly. In addition, no police checks were carried out, there was a delay in providing a social worker and the council failed to respond to give details of its complaints procedures despite a clear request to do so. It was also said that the foster carer and the teenage girl suffered anxiety over finance and that the latter lost education opportunities. The council agreed to pay £500 to the foster carer and £200 to the teenage girl (*Community Care*, 2001).

An example of what a proactive authority can achieve is shown by the example of Gloucestershire.

But the argument for keeping private foster carers on board by not toughening legislation and thereby not pushing private fostering underground overlooks one very obvious fact – private fostering is, very largely and in all places, an underground activity now. Anyone whose interest in children was less than well intentioned could not do better than take them into their home when their parents may be hundreds of miles away or not even in the same country and could, with impunity, not inform the local authority whose inspectorial function is, anyway, fairly perfunctory.

Proactive authorities

An example of what a proactive authority can achieve is shown by the example of Gloucestershire. Three years ago, the authority appointed Brendan McGrath as its Private Fostering Co-ordinator. His approach is the carrot not the stick. 'What you have to say,' he says, 'is: "We are going to help you" and not adopt a punitive approach.'

His approach is community based and he is also willing to be flexible in his interpretation of the law. As he says: 'The question is – is our role to safeguard children or to interpret the law to the letter?' Thus, when it comes to the 28-day rule, he says: 'I don't care about a day here or there.' To give another example of McGrath's flexibility, one organisation arranging visits for children from overseas, lodged them in hostels during the week and with host families at the weekend. 'Where would the children stay if they were ill?' he asked the organisers, and was told that the children would be full time with the host families. 'In which case', he argued, 'it would be a good idea to run the statutory checks on the families'.

CASELOAD IN SEPTEMBER 2001

Private fostering arrangements	15
Host families for holiday schemes	13
Host families for guardianship organisations	5
Host families for language schools	204

(The last three categories are listed as possibly falling within the Children Act 1989.)

Of the first category – private fostering arrangements – the 15 were broken down as follows:

Living with parents' ex foster carers	3
Living with family friends	2
Chinese babies privately fostered	3
Living with former childminder	1
Living with neighbour	1
Living with schoolfriend's family	1
Prior to intercountry adoption	1
Living with parent's former partner	2
Living with an older friend	1

The list of local contacts he makes to ensure that people know what private fostering is and what the legal responsibilities of parents and carers are is exhaustive: the citizen's advice bureaux; education social workers; Ukrainian social clubs and the local youth service; the police; churches; state, private and language schools; and organisations catering for members of local minority ethnic groups like the Bangladeshi women's group (with the exception of the already-mentioned Chinese children, almost all private fostering in Gloucestershire is of white children). He also invites representatives of all these agencies and organisations to the workshops which he runs.

On his principle (quoted earlier) of 'If you look, you find', McGrath's work is a good example of how cases will come to light. When he was appointed three years ago, there were 11 cases of private fostering known to the social services department. In 1999, the number had reached 30; a year later it was 78, which included, for the first time, 43 referrals from language schools. As of September this year (2001) the annual number was 224, with 189 from language schools (the box opposite shows September's caseload).

What is also impressive about McGrath's work is how the information which he has issued has been both very widely disseminated and has provoked this rise in numbers. This can be seen by the variety of people and agencies referring. In those three years they have gone from host families for home guardianship organisations and social services area teams to include hospital social workers, social services fostering workers, health visitors, education social workers, school nurses, foster carers, local state schools, language schools, parents, Citizens Advice Bureaux, educational psychologists and an NHS health trust. Every November, guardianship organisations send McGrath lists of children whom they have boarded out in Gloucestershire.

Language schools (which can be accredited by the British Council) in the county offer their children feedback sheets and give guidance to host families about single rooms. The schools would not, say, place two 15-year-old girls with a host family which had older teenage brothers.

Lincolnshire is currently reviewing practice and procedures, a review which will also be a prelude to a public awareness campaign.

Lincolnshire is another authority with a long interest in private fostering. It is currently reviewing practice and procedures, a review which will also be a prelude to a public awareness campaign. Two important changes which it plans are to strengthen assessment and reviewing. This will be done, first, by having family placement staff, experienced in home studies, undertaking assessments rather than social workers based in local teams. Second, reviews of placements will be carried out by the independent chairpersons of the council's looked-after children's reviews, rather than by a local team social worker and his or her manager.

The N'Deagainsia Project

I could discover only one voluntary agency which was working specifically with private foster carers. (As mentioned, the San Jai Project in Glasgow knew of the private fostering of Chinese children but did not have the capacity to work with them.) The N'Deagainsia Project (this is a Mende word meaning "caring for children") is jointly run by NCH and Plymouth and District Council for Racial Equality, and became operational in May. It is funded by the local health action zone and a Single Regeneration Fund grant to work with black children – a term which includes Chinese, Asian, African-Caribbean, African, Arab and Vietnamese. Children who are of mixed ethnicity are also within the project's purview.

While its work is now broader than wishing to work with children who are privately fostered and

FRANZ

Uschi and Dietrich Vogt were approved foster carers to Franz in their native Hamburg. When they came to live in England for work purposes, the German local authority wrote to International Social Service in London to ask the social services department, in whose area of London the Vogts were living, to continue to supervise the arrangement. (Germany retains a formal interest in its citizens even if they live abroad but relies on authorities in the countries to which they have gone to live to carry out any obligations which may be necessary in the case of matters like, for example, fostering.) Although the German fostering arrangement was not recognised here, it would be deemed private fostering in this country. But the local authority seemed oblivious to this fact. It turned down the request on the grounds that it was the German authority's responsibility and it should make its own arrangements.

their carers, its origins lie in the concerns raised about that group of children by a few locally active Sierra Leonese. They wanted to form a support group for the children in such care. Plymouth is another of those areas which raises especial problems for West African children who are being privately fostered: isolation from other black children; carers who have little idea of their cultural needs; carers wanting to avoid any statutory intervention and not registering the children with local GPs; and occasional issues about child protection. All of this cuts off some of the carers who will be among the city's poorest citizens.

fostering by asking local authorities to 'satisfy themselves that the arrangements are satisfactory and that foster carers are suitable. They do not approve or register private foster carers.' It is up to the local authority to decide how it indicates that it is satisfied without actually giving approval. Thus, private carers know that they have been checked but 'are left wondering about the conclusions', say Woollard and Clarke.

The peculiar irony of this over-emphasis on privacy is that, when private foster carers make applications for residence or adoption orders, then this *does* become a matter of concern for the state.

It is a curiosity of the persistence of this *laisser faire* approach to this aspect of social policy in the minds of legislators that the obvious needs to be stated in rebuttal after a century of interventionist legislation. The closest analogy to arguments about private fostering, as has been previously stated, is that of the registration of childminders, now 30 years past. This, too, is a private arrangement that also meets Holman's definition of the transaction quoted at the beginning of this report. Not so far removed either, by way of analogy, is the registration and inspection of independent nursery schools and playgroups. In all these cases, the children spend, at most, hours a day away from their parents; privately fostered children may be in the care of someone else for months, even years.

Turning to another aspect of "private" life where the law has intervened, it is not many years ago that a husband could not be prosecuted for raping his wife on the basis that this was an interference too far with domestic life. Again, while smacking in the UK has not been banned, nevertheless some punishments by parents of children that were a century ago regarded as reasonable chastisement are now subject to prosecution. And, of course, the Children Act 1989, with its central tenet of regard for 'the best interests of the child', does not recognise parents' interests as superior to those of children.

The peculiar irony of this over-emphasis on privacy is that, when private foster carers make applications for residence or adoption orders, then this *does* become a matter of concern for the state.

ADENIKE

Adenike came to the UK from Nigeria when she was 10, the eldest of three children. Her private foster carers in a white area of Kent were unknown to her and her brother and sister before they met and they were told nothing about them by her mother. While her immediate reaction to her new home was 'I hate this', she was quickly diverted to surviving and especially to protecting the other two children.

Her education was affected by problems with the language. Survival was uppermost in her mind – her parents, she felt, had abandoned her and it had fallen to her to care for her brother and sister.

Two months after Adenike came to live in Kent her foster father was sexually abusing her. To cope she pretended it was not happening; her body was not her body. The children felt scared, lost and abandoned with no-one to turn to. The people who were supposed to look after them were abusing them. They were told that if they said anything they would be sent back to Africa. The shocking images of children starving during the Biafran war, which was then being waged, constantly reminded them of why they had to survive what was happening to them.

After two years, payments to the foster carers stopped, provoking the involvement of social services. But when the social worker called, she never spoke to the children on their own.

Today Adenike finds relating to others difficult, especially to her husband and children. She finds difficulty in demonstrating her love for them physically. In foster care she could not show her emotions. Periodically she has nightmares of the daily sexual abuse she knew in the private foster home. Sleepless nights, flashbacks and the insecurity of fearing being left alone are reminders and consequences of her past young life.

(Based on Clarke, 1999)

8 A very public practice

How a few local authorities have positively dealt with private fostering shows what can be done by adopting a proactive rather than a minimalist approach. However, some authorities, which have done a lot, have still trimmed what they do against what the DoH guidance expects of them; they cut their practice coat according to their resources cloth. Oxfordshire, for example, which, as has been mentioned, has worked very closely with language schools, does not, among other things, routinely carry out health checks on private foster carers; it does not interview even one of the two carers' referees unless a reference causes concern; and nor does it meet the DoH's expectation that young people who have been privately fostered will continue to receive services from social workers if desired. As its own guidance states, summing up the view of many other local authorities: 'Oxfordshire is struggling to meet the needs of young people whom it looks after and expects parents to exercise responsibility for young children who have been privately fostered' (Oxfordshire County Council, May 1998).

Improvements in local authority practice
What, then, could local authorities do now in the absence of any change in the law?

● Private foster carers should be made aware that, in certain circumstances, they can benefit from Section 17 assistance for children deemed to be "in need" – this could be cash or a range of services. They may also be eligible for social security payments such as Child Benefit and possibly Income Support or Job Seekers Allowance if in receipt of Child Benefit.

● Local networks for local authority foster carers should not just be foster networks of those registered with the local authority but should include private carers who could be offered

How a few local authorities have positively dealt with private fostering shows what can be done by adopting a proactive rather than a minimalist approach.

training and support alongside local authority foster carers. Help might include making available ethnically appropriate toys and books; information about food, skin care and health, and the child's culture; assisting carers to meet with black families or others who are caring for black children.

● All local authorities should mount publicity campaigns informing carers and parents what their obligations are in law and what support is available. But such campaigns could be more effective if aimed with certain groups in mind. For example, Oxfordshire has done much work with language schools, including a dedicated leaflet because children attending those schools are the largest group of privately fostered children in the county. Leaflets and posters should be made available in public places, GP surgeries, health centres, libraries and schools.

● Local authorities should draft model agreements as guides for parents and carers.

● In the absence of formal registration, local authorities could keep informal lists of carers whom they have visited and regard as satisfactory and, importantly, those who have been barred from taking children.

- Social workers should liaise with colleagues in the areas from which children come to facilitate not only their entry back into their families but also their re-entry or entry into the local school system.

- There should be greater co-ordination to identify the children between social services and education departments, health authorities, voluntary agencies and the police.

- In terms of their practice, social services can crack down on private foster carers because they believe that private fostering is a bad thing *per se*. Or they can see the carers as partners in child care and seek to support them as they would their own foster carers (which is not to say, of course, that they should not use their powers of prohibition to the full where justified). One consequence of the first approach is that those foster carers who are capable of improving what they do with help, might give up and parents would then be forced to find another carer. The child would be moved again and the care might not be as good.

Angus Geddes refers to four groups of carers. For the first – the bad ones, the Section 1 offenders and those whose own children have been removed from them – he says that the law is strong enough to prohibit them. Second, there are carers providing high standards of care. A third group are those who provide a standard of care that is adequate but who could be helped to raise their standards if a local authority devotes some resources to them. The last group are those about whom at the moment very little can be done – they provide poor care and are never going to improve but the children are never with them long enough for much to be done about them. That group, Geddes thinks, would disappear with registration.

As it is, social workers are too often faced with accepting what is just about acceptable care. As Jackie Oldfield, Service Manager, Havant & Petersfield, Hampshire County Council, said of her days as a social worker: 'It was hellish trying to come to terms with what was good enough when something really had to be bad enough to remove the children.'

'It was hellish trying to come to terms with what was good enough when something really had to be bad enough to remove the children.'

9 Towards a better future

Parents who have their children privately fostered are no different, in one important respect, from many other parents – what they want is affordable, efficient, flexible child care. This would allow *all* parents to make free and informed choices about their children's care. Where they differ from other parents is that what is available – nurseries, state and private, or childminders – does not suit their needs.

The battle for universally available child care is a long one which has yet to be won despite the promises of successive governments. However, as it is impossible to imagine, other than in an ideal world, arrangements which would suit *every* parent's needs, some parents are always likely to want to enter into an arrangement with someone else, often a stranger, who is willing to look after their child.

The DoH guidance (Department of Health, 1991) makes a crucial point: 'The main similarity between local authority family placements and private fostering is the nature of the experience for the child.'

The potential for abuse is all too obvious and the death of Victoria Climbié brought it to public attention. One unfortunate consequence of her death would be if it were seen, to both legislators and the general public, as "just" another child death tragedy, with recommendations being made about the tightening of procedures, the need for greater co-operation between agencies, and all the recommendations which have peppered almost every report since the inquiry into the death of Maria Colwell in 1974. All of these may well prove necessary in the light of the findings of the Laming Inquiry.

However, Victoria's death was different from others in one significant regard – it was the death of a privately fostered child. Children have been removed because of the danger of both sexual and physical abuse (African Family Advisory Service, 1991). But Victoria's death is the first of a privately fostered child to be the subject of an inquiry, either one held by a local authority or the Government. The reasons why she came to this country also illustrate one of the reasons, frequently referred to above, why West African parents often enlist others to care for their children. It is true that Victoria was unusual in that she was in the charge of a family member (but not one recognised by the law governing private fostering). Also, she was not, like so many West African children, placed with a white person hitherto unknown to her parents. However, her parents' intention in entrusting her to her great-aunt was the hope of a better life and the promise of a first-class education. Marie Thérèse Kouao visited the family and said that she was willing to take one of the children to Europe. As the child's father, Francis, was to tell the Laming inquiry: 'This was a huge proposal for us and everyone was smiling' (quoted, Carvel, 2001). When, two days later, Victoria left her home she was seen off by all her extended family and neighbours. Francis Climbié went on to state: 'I have been asked whether I lay any blame to myself for handing over Victoria in this way and I can say I do not because it's a custom for people to be taken to Europe … I think she would have succeeded brilliantly.'

There are enormous complications surrounding Victoria's death which touch upon professional competence, the management of public authorities, the ability of agencies to co-operate effectively, and the resources available to public services to do their work. Within this, it would be easy to lose sight of one aspect of all this – Victoria's status as a privately fostered child. But it is an important one and should be held on to. It is true that a tougher regulatory regime for private fostering might not have saved Victoria but it has shown, in extreme and tragic form, the risks that privately fostered children are exposed to.

Much remains the same

One of the most striking things about private foster care is that, despite the advent of the Children Act 1989, which dramatically influenced and changed many aspects of the child care system, so much remains the same. For example, in 1988, the African Family Advisory Service (quoted in Atkinson and Horner, 1990) undertook a survey of ten local authorities and looked in-depth at three of them. It found what any similar survey would find today, some of which is confirmed by experience, some by work which has been carried out. Among other things, AFAS discovered that:

- local authorities and foster carers had little or no knowledge of the children's backgrounds, their medical history or how long the placements would last;

- the children were often passed from one local foster carer to the next;

- local authorities had difficulty keeping track of children's movements between authorities;

- children suffered behavioural and other problems due to unsatisfactory placements;

- there were problems in introducing children back into their families;

The shortcomings identified in the DoH inspections of 1993 are likely to be confirmed by the inspections carried out earlier this year.

The problem is not merely that local authorities have the powers but fail to use them. It is the case that local authorities do not, for the most part, exercise what powers they do have with much commitment.

- all the West African children were with white carers who showed little understanding of their cultural and identity needs; and

- many carers offered low physical and emotional standards of care.

The shortcomings identified in the DoH inspections of 1993 (Department of Health, 1994) are likely to be confirmed by the inspections carried out earlier this year. Not only did those inspections find ignorance of the regulations, legislation and guidance and a lack of preparedness by local authorities to deal with private fostering, but the report referred to 'potentially vulnerable children … being placed in the care of strangers, without any checks being undertaken as to their suitability to care for children'. The report added: 'The way in which some placements were being made raised very real concerns about the welfare of the children.' Two years later, Utting (1997) expressed 'considerable anxiety' and said that this was an area 'where children are not being safeguarded properly, indeed an unknown number are likely to be seriously at risk'.

In 1971, Middleton wrote, in his history of child care in the first half of the last century, of privately fostered children covered by the Public Health Act 1936 and the Public Health Act (London) 1937, that information about them was 'non-existent' and that there was 'ample opportunity for indifferent child care'. He could say exactly the same today.

The need for registration

As it is hoped that this report has shown, the problem is not merely that local authorities have the powers but fail to use them. It is the case that local authorities do not, for the most part, exercise what powers they do have with much commitment. But also they do not have the most fundamental power which is critical to allowing them to use more effectively the powers that they do possess. This power would also reveal what local authorities and government do not know at the moment – how widespread is the practice of private fostering. The power which local authorities need is that to approve and register private foster carers.

At present, social services departments need only to satisfy themselves of the child's welfare, and only in the most extreme cases are they able to remove a child or to prevent a child being given into the care of a private foster carer. There is, then, a dangerous inequality in the way that local authorities are charged to deal with those foster carers whom they recruit and register and those who offer a private service. Indeed, there is a damaging inequality between the way privately fostered children are viewed and children who are looked after by the local authority, a point made specifically by the SSI in the report of the 1993 inspections (Department of Health, 1994). A local authority wishing to remove a child from the home of a private foster carer can only do so by application to a court; in the case of one its own foster carers the child can be removed under emergency procedures immediately – thus, the private foster carer is placed on par, legally, with a birth parent. This is because the authority of the private foster carer comes direct from the birth parent. This is not an open and shut argument but it is one which, in part, revolves around how "private" private fostering can be regarded by the state.

Another of the many anomalies and inequalities affecting privately fostered children and children in the care of local authorities is that Quality Protects, which did not include privately fostered children, seeks to reduce to three the number of moves to which a child in care can be subject. Privately fostered children are excluded from such considerations and are often moved without even their parents' knowledge.

Not knowing who private foster carers are militates against local authorities using their powers. For some it is the excuse to do nothing because they believe that there is nothing to be done. It enables them to play down the potential problems. This is dangerous reasoning. For it not only allows any private fostering which does exist to go unchecked, but where a neighbouring authority attempts to weed out unsatisfactory carers because it is proactive, either carers will move to the inactive authority's area or cause the children to be moved.

In 1993, the British Association of Social Workers' survey showed that 50 per cent of the responding local authorities considered that they were not fulfilling their statutory duties towards privately fostered children. BASW's view was that health visitors were filling the gap in statutory services (Jones, 1993).

Government no longer claims, as it did only a decade ago, that the number of placements is falling, as if that, in any case, was relevant to protecting children. But what we can say is that the highest estimates, based as they are on guesswork and a paucity of statistical information, are likely to be lower than the actual numbers. Services for children in private foster care, for their carers and their parents are the most under-resourced and neglected of all child care services. In some places they are non-existent. And because, too, local authorities do not have the power of registration and approval, they tend not to place much stress on offering a comprehensive service – or, in some places, any service at all.

Utting (1997) said that there were three options – to leave things as they were; to de-regulate on the basis that what existed was unenforceable; or to enforce regulation because of the risk to children. The status quo, he went on to say, was 'the worst of all worlds as it seems to give the appearance of safeguards while in practice they are not complied with'. Deregulation would 'abandon children to their fate' and create a '"honey pot" for abusers'.

Utting's third option – to enforce regulation, which is the DoH attitude – would, he believed, place upon social services departments 'commitments they cannot realistically fulfil'. However, when Utting opted for approval and registration, he did see, as he told me, that there would be resource implications. But to have done otherwise, he added, would have been illogical given the registration of providers of day care, where the numbers are larger than those of children privately fostered. He also believed that registration would 'mop up' issues about children in language schools, where, he said, concerns had been expressed to his inquiry.

The most recent advocate for change was the UK Joint Working Party on Foster Care, whose work led to the adoption of the National Foster Care Standards. It included representatives of English, Welsh and Scottish local authorities, BAAF, the National Foster Care Association, the Local Government Association, the Association of Directors of Social Services and the Association of Directors of Social Work, and the National Children's Bureau, along with academic and (local authority) foster care members.

Its report (UK Joint Working Party on Foster Care, 1999) referred to Utting's concerns about abuse and said that 'the high potential for abuse and neglect' had to be taken 'more seriously by the government'. It went on to say that the regulations that existed 'are seldom enforced'. It came to the conclusion that:

Utting said that there were three options – to leave things as they were; to de-regulate on the basis that what existed was unenforceable; or to enforce regulation because of the risk to children.

Government should investigate, as a matter of urgency, the extent of private foster arrangements and the quality of care being provided. If, as anticipated, the standards revealed are not satisfactory, it should then bring forward legislation at the earliest opportunity to introduce registration of private foster carers and regulate and monitor private fostering arrangements. It should also provide necessary resources required by authorities to enforce such regulation and regularly inspect to ensure its enforcement.

Thus, the vital missing piece in the jigsaw which is private fostering, is registration.

It should be a criminal offence to foster children privately unless carers are approved by, and placed on a register kept by the local authority. It should also be a criminal offence to place children for private fostering with someone who is not on the register.

Caring for other people's children – in local authority foster care and through adoption – is notoriously complex and shot through with often contradictory assumptions and expectations. Private fostering raises many of these issues and more. It places vulnerable children into the care of people who may be well intentioned but insensitive to their needs; or whose motives for looking after a child may be, at best, questionable and, at worst, sinister. These children may be separated from their parents by hundreds and, in some cases, thousands of miles. Thrown into this pot, too, are the position of parents who lose their children through the courts and the attachment of their children to people to whose care they were entrusted with no thought that those people might eventually offer the child a permanent home.

To support and assist those private foster carers who are capable of good care, is to place new demands on hard-pressed local authorities. For the practitioner, going about his or her daily business, the task is to practice in a sea of complexity. But none of this is an argument to leave matters where they are. Where matters are is where they have been for three decades, despite changes in the law and developments in child care practice and our understanding of children's needs. That Victoria Climbié might still have died had registration been on the statute book is not the point – no system is infallible. The compelling criticism of the present system of protecting privately fostered children is that, for all intents and purposes, it is hardly more effective than it was 20 years before she was born.

Thus, the vital missing piece in the jigsaw which is private fostering, is registration. It should be a criminal offence to foster children privately unless carers are approved by, and placed on a register kept by the local authority.

A programme for reform

Action for Central Government

1. Legislation should be introduced to require local authorities to maintain a register of private foster carers within their area who are approved as suitable. This register would be available to birth parents who wished to make arrangements for their child. It should be possible for a private foster carer to be registered as generally available or alternatively to be approved for a specific child already known to them in the same way that foster carers can be approved to foster a specific child.

2. It should be an offence to foster a child privately if the carer is unregistered or to place a child with an unregistered carer.

3. Each local authority should be required to make an annual statistical return to the Department of Health detailing the number of private foster carers registered, the number deregistered, and the number of placements in its area.

4. Standards should be published by the Department of Health with the criteria against which private foster carers should be assessed for registration. These should be based on current standards for childminders and include elements of the National Standards for Foster Care.

5. The National Care Standards commission should be required to inspect the private fostering service of Local Authorities in England and Wales as already required in Scotland.

6. The Children Act 1989 should be amended to make explicit that the stipulation of 28 days as the period after which the child is deemed to be privately fostered need not be continuous.

7. Each local authority should be required to appoint a designated social work manager with specific responsibility for private fostering overall.

8. Local authorities should have a statutory duty to provide counselling and advice to birth parents considering having their child privately fostered.

9. The local authority should have a duty to offer support to young people who were in private foster care three months before their 16th birthday.

10. Private foster carers who have children removed from their care by the Local Authority should be notified to the Protection of Children Act List.

11. The Government should have a continuing campaign, backing any efforts by local authorities, to inform professionals, birth parents and private foster carers of their legal responsibilities.

12. A Code of Practice should be published by the Department of Health to recognise the differing circumstances of children who are privately fostered, for example, those in host families when on vacation from independent schools; those attending summer schools; those in the UK for medical treatment.

13. Private fostering should be integral to all relevant Government initiatives addressed at improving services for children, for example, the Quality Protects Programme.

Action by Local Authorities/Social Services Departments

1. Each authority should address private fostering specifically in its Children's Services Plan.

2. The principles of the Children Act 1989 – including the need to consider a child's religion, race, culture and langugae – should be incorporated in all local authority guidelines and policies on private fostering.

3. Local authorities should treat private foster carers as part of the spectrum of local childcare and ensure that they are supported and knowledgeable about assistance and benefits to which they may be entitled.

4. Private fostering arrangements should always be the subject of a written contract between parents and foster carers.

5. Written contracts should detail access by the child to the parents and local authorities should satisfy themselves that the amount of contact may allow the child to maintain an attachment to his or her parents. Local authorities should therefore bear in mind their duties under schedule 2 paragraph 10 of the Children Act, to promote contact between children in need living apart from their family and the family.

6. The local authority should satisfy itself that the care will be for a stated period although that can be extended by mutual consent of the parent and the carer. Parents should be informed, in detail and in writing, by the local authority of the possible consequences of private fostering for their children and their relationship with their children.

7. Local authorities that become aware of a privately fostered child who has moved from another local authority area with his/her private carer should be required to inform their previous local authority.

8. A local authority which is aware of the intention of a private carer to move outside the area should inform the receiving authority.

9. Professionals, for example, GPs, Health Visitors, Teachers, Housing Officers – should have a duty to inform the social services department when they suspect a child is being privately fostered.

Executive summary

- The term "private fostering" is used to describe the situation when a child of up to 16 years of age (18 if disabled) is in the care of someone who is not his or her parent or relative for 28 days or more. A relative, under the Children Act 1989, is defined as grandparents, siblings, step-parents, aunts or uncles (i.e. brothers or sisters of the child's parents), or other persons with parental responsibility.

- Some parents will always need to make use of private foster care. But the needs of their children for support, protection and a healthy physical and emotional development are no different from those of any other children.

- Privately fostered children include children placed with strangers for lengthy periods, often while their parents pursue studies, work commitments or live overseas; adolescents who are temporarily estranged from their families; children who attend language schools and independent schools in the UK; children from abroad on holiday or exchange visits; children who are asylum seekers; and some children brought to the UK from overseas with a view to adoption.

- As there is no register of private foster carers, families have to find these carers themselves. They may do this through word of mouth or informal networks. The Department of Health says that parents are responsible for ensuring that the people they place their children with are suitable. However, parents have no access to criminal record checks and most will have little understanding of the possible risks that their children face.

- There is no accurate information about the numbers of children who are privately fostered. Current estimates suggest that 8 – 10,000 children are privately fostered in the UK, a significant majority of whom are black children of West African origin. The Department of Health ceased to collect statistics in 1990 on the grounds that they were meaningless.

- The majority of privately fostered West African children live with white families, often in rural communities where the child will experience separation from his or her culture and may encounter racism. Many private foster carers have little understanding of the difficulties these children may face or the impact on them of separation from their birth families. The long-term effects can be a confusion about identity, relationship problems, underachievement, insecurity, poor development, and learning difficulties.

- Some West African families have lost their children when they have been adopted by private foster carers or when children have become so detached from their parents to not want to, or be able to, return to them.

- The Children Act 1989 introduced changes in England and Wales. These were to place a duty on both carer and birth parent to notify an intention to place a child in private foster care, and limiting the numbers of children whom a carer could foster to three. Despite these duties, it is generally accepted that the great majority of private fostering arrangements are never notified to the authorities.

- Local authorities have fairly minimal responsibilities under the Children Act 1989. Essentially, they have to satisfy themselves about the welfare of the child; receive notification from parents, carers, and third parties; visit the child regularly and offer advice and support. They do not have the power to approve private foster carers and have only limited powers to prohibit a person from privately fostering.

- The overwhelming majority of social services departments do not give any priority to privately fostered children. In many cases, no services are provided in the belief that there are no such children within the authority's boundaries. A few local authorities have developed good practice initiatives and have actively promoted services to meet the needs of privately fostered children in their area.

- There is a dangerous inequality in the way that local authorities are charged to deal with those foster carers whom they recruit and register for children in the local authority's care and those who offer a private service. The statutory requirement and regulatory framework which apply to child minders who will look after children for part of the day, are much more rigorous than for children who can be separated from their parents for indefinite periods.

- Sir William Utting, in his review of the safeguards for children living away from home (1997), said that there were three options: to leave things as they were; to deregulate on the basis that what existed was unenforceable; or to enforce regulation and introduce a requirement to approve and register private foster carers because of the risk to children. He said that the status quo was 'the worst of all worlds as it seems to give the appearance of safeguards while in practice they are not complied with'. Deregulation would 'abandon children to their fate' and create a '"honeypot" for abusers'. He recommended that private foster carers should be approved in the same way as other foster carers.

- The recommendations for change made by Sir William Utting in his report – which was commissioned by Government – were rejected in 1998. Almost all Utting's other recommendations were accepted by Government. The UK Joint Working Party on Foster Care in their report in 1999 referred to the 'high potential for abuse and neglect' and urged legislation requiring local authorities to maintain a register of approved private foster carers at the earliest opportunity. The Government instead promised a public awareness campaign which would take place in 1999. The only "campaign" to date has been a distribution of leaflets to professionals and letters to Directors reminding them of their responsibilities.

- BAAF's investigative report, written by Terry Philpot, highlights graphically the risks to which privately fostered children are exposed, providing powerful case study material and making urgent recommendations for Government actions to ensure these children are protected.

- In 2001, Victoria Climbié, a privately fostered child, died tragically at the hands of her carer and her carer's partner.

References

Afolabi O, (November 1990) 'Private fostering: Whose interest is served?', *Nigerian News*

African Family Advisory Service (1991) *Private Fostering: The need to safeguard, protect and promote*, London: Save the Children

African Family Advisory Service (1997) *Private Fostering: Development of policy and practice in three English local authorities*, London: Save the Children

Association of Directors of Social Services (2001) *ADSS Survey February 2001: Local authorities and private fostering*, ADSS

Atkinson C and Horner A (1990) 'Private Fostering: Legislation and practice,' *Adoption & Fostering*, 14:3

Black Bag (1996) BBC2

Black Britain (1997) BBC2

Boswell J (1991) *The Kindness of Strangers*, London: Penguin

Carvel J (29 September, 2001) 'Climbié parents tell of alarm at "sad" pictures', *The Guardian*

Clarke B (ed) (1999) *A Seminar and Workshop for Professionals Working in a Multicultural Community with a Focus on Private Fostering*, Privately published

Community Care, (10–16 May, 2001) 'Lancashire failed to act', *Community Care*

Department of Health (1991) *The Children Act 1989 Guidance and Regulations. Volume 8. Private Fostering and Miscellaneous*, and *The Children (Private Arrangements for Fostering) Regulations 1991*, London: HMSO

Department of Health (1994) *Signposts: Findings from a national inspection of private fostering*, London: Department of Health

Department of Health, (1998) *The Government's Response to the Children's Safeguards Review*, London: The Stationery Office

Department of Health (2001) *Private Fostering: A cause for concern*, London: Department of Health, http://www.doh.gov.uk/scg/privatefostering/index.htm

Hampshire County Council (15 September 1993) Report of the Director of Social Services to the Children and Social Services Sub-Committee, Hampshire County Council

Holman R (1973) *Trading in Children: A study of private fostering*, London: Routledge & Kegan Paul

Holman R (15 January 2001) Letter, *The Guardian*

Israel S and McVeigh T (23 September 2001) 'What happened to Victoria will happen to someone else', *The Observer*

Jones D (22 June 1993) Letter to W. Rose, Assistant Chief Inspector of Social Services, Department of Health

Leisham J (1980) *The Nigerian Family in Britain*, Unpublished PhD thesis, University of Ibadan, Nigeria

Maximé E J (1993) 'The importance of racial identity for the psychological well-being of black children', *Acpp Review & Newsletter*, 15:4

McGrath B (2001a) Unpublished notes for workshop participants

McGrath B (2001b) Correspondence with the author

Middleton J (1971) *When Family Failed*, London: Gollancz

Nesbitt A (1990) 'The African child and his family in an inner London health authority', Unpublished MSc thesis

Oxfordshire County Council (May 1998) *Children Cared for Away from Home, Guidance Paper Three: Private fostering procedures*, Oxfordshire County Council

Race Equality Unit (1993) *Black Children and Private Fostering*, London: Race Equality Unit

Triseliotis J, Sellick C and Short R (1995) *Foster Care: Theory and practice*, London: BT Batsford in association with BAAF, 1995

UK Joint Working Party on Foster Care (1999) *Report and Recommendations*, London: National Foster Care Association

Utting W (1997) *People Like Us: The report of the review of the safeguards for children living away from home*, London: The Stationery Office

Woollard C and Clarke B (1999), 'Private fostering', in Wheal A (ed), *The RHP Companion to Foster Care*, Lyme Regis: Russell House Publishing

Woollard C (1991) 'Private Fostering: A health concern', *Adoption & Fostering*, 15:3

Useful reading

In addition to many of the references listed above, readers will find the following of practical use:

BAAF (1996) *Private Fostering*, London: BAAF

Batty D (ed) (1995) with the Private Fostering Special Interest Group of the Health Visitors Association, *Caring for Other People's Children: A guide for private foster carers*, London: BAAF

Batty D with Wrighton P (1996) *Your Child and Private Foster Care: A guide for birth parents considering private fostering*, London: BAAF